Miracle Working Faith

Tommy Ray O'Dell

Harrison House
Tulsa, OK

16 15 14   5 4 3 2 1

Miracle Working Faith

ISBN: 978-160683-883-4

Copyright © 2014 by Tommy Ray O'Dell

Published by:

Harrison House Publishers

Tulsa, OK 74145

Dedication

This book is dedicated to all believers who sincerely desire to be used of God. The secrets shared within this book will unlock the mysteries that have helped my wife, Elisabeth, and me share the Good News with millions globally. For almost three decades, we have gone to the most neglected and unreached people groups of the world, seeing audiences of up to 150,000 pray to receive Jesus in a single night.

This book contains many of the greatest truths that we have witnessed face-to-face in more than seventy nations. We dedicate this book, investing these truths into your life and ministry. Jesus is the same in you! Remember, all things are possible if you only believe.

I also want to dedicate this book to my beloved grandfather, mentor and friend, Dr. T.L. Osborn. He was a missionary evangelist to the unreached world and was best known for his mass-miracle ministry. He and my grandmother, Dr. Daisy Osborn, proclaimed the Gospel to millions of unreached people around the world. I greatly miss them and dedicate my life to continuing in their footsteps until the day I die.

Contents

Prologue 1

Chapter 1 One Man, One Mission 5

Chapter 2 What Is Faith? 23

Chapter 3 What Is Ministry? 35

Chapter 4 The Key Ingredient 53

Chapter 5 I Believe in Miracles Because I Am a Miracle 61

Chapter 6 Know Your Enemy 71

Chapter 7 Confessions of Power 83

Chapter 8 People Are Eternal 89

Chapter 9 Hindu Hostilities and Muslim Miracles 99

Chapter 10 Miracles Reveal 111

Epilogue The Road Less Traveled 119

Prayer 121

Poems, Song Lyrics 122

Remembering T.L. Osborn 147

Prologue

The Life and Ministry of My Grandfather, T.L. Osborn.

Wow, What a legacy. I'm so honored to be one of the ministers influenced by my grandfather. He revolutionized my life. He was my hero, my mentor, my friend, and my confidante. Sometimes we philosophied together. He was also the Encourager in Chief.

When we returned from a crusade, he was like a little boy, excited to hear about every miracle and all the great things God had done. He preached the gospel to more people face-to-face than anyone who has ever lived. He was a soul winner. The Bible says in Daniel, "Those who are wise shall shine like the brightness of the firmament, and those that turn many to righteousness like the stars forever and ever." Oh! his reward is great. "What is our hope or joy or crown of rejoicing. Is it not even you in the presence of our lord Jesus Christ at his coming."

He was my strongest ally, my hero, and my example. He was the one who taught me how to be courageous. No one was more courageous than T.L. Osborn. In his whole life, he never hit anybody, he never threw anybody and he never wrestled anybody, but he was a warrior.

Look at the millions upon millions of lives that have been impacted through the life of T.L. Osborn and Frontier Evangelism. I look around and see some of the greatest men and women of God who have ever lived. And I think about how we were all influenced, how we were changed, and how our hearts were encouraged and challenged by T.L. Osborn.

When I think about him, all I think about is this young guy from the farm who saw Jesus. He didn't have any education; he left school in the 8th grade. Nevertheless, he never stopped learning, he never stopped pushing, and he never stopped growing. He never peaked. He loved people. His generosity and love for people everywhere was always on display.

One of the sweetest things I remember about him was that anytime he would come off the airplane and there was someone working at the airport in a lowly position, who rushed up saying, "T.L. Osborn, I know you," he would stop and treat them like royalty. He lived what he preached. He was a man of love. He had the most amazing gift for making everyone he met feel like they were his best friend. Now, actually, I was his best friend.

His compassion for the most forgotten is something that I, with all my heart, want to emulate. I want to be like grandpa. His passion to bring the Message of the Gospel to every unreached soul was never quenched. He never deviated from that purpose. He was like a laser, targeted on the purpose of reaching the unreached. He never faltered. His theme was Jesus Christ is the same yesterday today, and forever. That's what he lived, that's what he preached, and that's what he demonstrated. I'll never forget when I was in Ireland. As a young preacher, I had just been delivered from drugs, my burned out mind healed instantly. I was on the streets but I received Jesus and the power of God poured through me like fire and I was transformed.

When I went to my grandpa and told him my story, he told me it was the greatest miracle he had ever seen in his whole life. When I was preaching in Ireland after that, and thought I had preached a great sermon, he came up to me and said, "I think that's one of the greatest sermons I've ever heard, but now you've got to demonstrate it. You just finished your sermon and said, "The end." You can't do that." He told me: "Always preach truth, because truth will always demonstrate. And if you can't demonstrate it, you're not fit to preach it." From that day, I never preach anywhere, whether it's to a crowd of a hundred thousand people or just a handful of folks, where I don't demonstrate what I preach.

We have all benefited from the pioneer spirit of my grandfather. In the modern era, he was the first one to do mass campaigns, and miracle films, while giving away a ton of Gospel literature every day. He was a tireless warrior against racism, sexism, and classism. The theme of his ministry was, "You can do it too." Now it is our time to demonstrate the risen Christ. He has passed the baton on to us.

I am T.L. Osborn's grandson; I am his seed. We cannot stop! We have preached to millions of people over a period of thirty years in eight nations. However, I would not have done anything or known anything if it weren't for T.L. Osborn. He was My friend, my ally, and last but not least, my grandpa. I love you!

Chapter 1

One Man, One Mission

When I was sixteen, my mind was ravaged with drugs. My life was ruined. My family had given up on me. They didn't expect me to make it to my seventeenth birthday. I grew up in church. In fact, my grandparents are the well-known missionary evangelists, T.L. and Daisy Osborn. But even though I had been raised by wonderful believers, I personally had not yet surrendered my life to Jesus.

Most of the people in the world haven't had many chances to know Jesus. I had so many opportunities, but I missed a lot of them. God was compassionate to me. I started getting involved with drugs when I was fourteen years old. By the time I was fifteen, I was heavily involved in them. I took LSD, angel dust and every chemical I could get my hands on. I was reckless, just cooking my brain.

If I had been God, I wouldn't have wanted anything to do with me. Some people can do drugs and still maintain an appearance of normalcy for a long time. That seems incredible to me because I was never like that. I was the kind of person who would see somebody do one hit, then go and do ten myself. You have probably known someone like this.

I had already burned out my brain by the time I was sixteen. I also got involved in Eastern mysticism and astral projection while trying to find peace. On three separate occasions I tried to commit suicide by overdosing, only abusing my body further with drugs in the process.

"Send Him to Africa"

My parents were at a loss—panicked! They didn't know what to do. They said, "We have to get him away from these bad elements in Tulsa. You know what we should do? We should send him to Africa." That may sound surprising to you, but as an international missions' family, we are a world family. We didn't think about borders much. My parents thought if I got away from peer pressure, everything would be fine. The only problem was I was the peer pressure! So sending me to Africa was the nicest thing they could have ever done for my friends.

My grandparents travelled all over the world evangelizing and had friends who were missionaries in Kenya, East Africa. Their missionary friends agreed that I could live with them, hoping this would straighten me out. But the truth is, when I got to Africa, I went from bad to worse. The devil is the same anywhere you go. We live in a mean, sinful world.

When I arrived in Africa, I discovered that a pharmaceutical I used to pay for grew wild there. The country was overrun with imported drugs! I switched from pot to opium. East Africa had a big population of Indians, so I became even more heavily involved with Eastern mysticism. But I saw something else while I was over there. I saw real believers. I had grown up in Pentecostal churches all my life, but the genuineness of the believers I saw in Africa really touched my heart. Yet, I still wasn't ready to surrender my life.

The missionaries finally gave up on me and ended up sending me home in defeat. There was nothing they could do with me because I lived like the devil. I overdosed on the way back home. When I landed, I was arrested and taken into the loving care of the Houston police department. I was a skinny guy with long hair, moccasins, army fatigues and a dashiki. The police just loved me; I was their kind of kid (just kidding). They eventually sent me home to Tulsa because they were unable to find any drugs on me—I had already consumed them all!

When I arrived at the airport, I blew off my parents and left with my old friends. I went on a chemical binge and ended up doing even more damage to my brain. Sometimes I did not even remember my own name. I slept wherever I passed out and woke up covered in my own vomit. I fasted for days and days, up to a week, because I knew if you didn't eat anything while taking drugs, they would have a lot stronger effect—especially hallucinogens. Not only would I forget about eating, I wouldn't drink water either. I only drank whiskey or any kind of alcohol I could get my hands on.

At sixteen years old, I looked like a walking corpse—a wasted old person with brown teeth, hair falling out, and brittle bones. My situation was grave. It seemed like there was no hope for me. Death seemed inescapable.

God Is in Charge

Even when I was at my worst, God was dealing with me. People were planting seeds. God was leading me on paths where I could hear the Gospel. Even though I was rejecting it, the Word was still being planted in my heart. The seeds that are planted in us at a young age will eventually bear fruit. The truths I heard my grandfather preach when I was a little boy still lived in my heart. Those seeds were working; they were still living in me.

One time I was with some friends late at night prowling through town in a beat-up car, high out of my mind. I had been taking a lot of different drugs that night. I took acid and other pills, smoked a lot of hash, and consumed vast quantities of alcohol. Then I overdosed.

My body started convulsing and my friends got scared. I actually felt my spirit leave my body. I looked down and saw my body. I was terrified! I went down a dark tunnel, pursued by something horrible and ghastly. Seized by panic, smothered by fear, I had terrifying visions of all kinds of weird demonic scenes.

Then Satan appeared. He didn't come in a red suit with horns. He came with his evil eyes, terrifying presence, and all-consuming darkness. He said, "If you serve me, Tommy, you can be a king in my kingdom. I'll give you whatever you want, whatever your heart desires."

I might have been ignorant, but that was the first time I ever dreamed I was serving the devil. Up to that moment, I always thought I was just doing my own thing, not hurting anyone, just trying to find another way to get to God.*

When the devil made his proposition, I said "No." Then I was plunged into hell. I felt myself being sucked out into a dark place where I did not want to go to. I don't know why I did it, how I did it, or where I did it, but I just screamed out, "Jesus!" And suddenly, I was back.

'I thought all paths led to the same destination. Proverbs 14:12 and 16:25 says, "There is a way *that seems* right to a man, but in the end it leads to death." (NIV, emphasis mine) Jesus is the only path to life. He is more than a religious concept or a philosopher promising peace. Jesus is truth! Jesus really lived. He really died. He really rose again. He is still living today! He is the only One who can lead us home to God.

In the meantime, my friends were freaking out. They thought that I was dead or going to die. But I came back. I tried to speak but the experience was so overwhelming, I couldn't. I just stuttered. My friends were scared because they thought they were going to get stuck with a corpse. Remember, these were my

---

* I thought all paths led to the same destination. Proverbs 14:12 and 16:25 says, "There is a way that seems right to a man, but in the end it leads to death." (NIV, emphasis mine) Jesus is the only path to life. He is more than a religious concept or a philosopher promising peace. Jesus is truth! Jesus really lived. He really died. He really rose again. He is still living today! He is the only One who can lead us home to God.

close friends—friends I had known for a long time. But they just stopped the car, pushed me out into the gutter, and drove away.

I pulled myself up and crawled around to the back of a vacant house. It was dark and cold. I looked up to pray. I didn't have enough brain cells left to carry on a conversation. I was like a burned-out animal, having no hope whatsoever. I looked up and prayed the best prayer I knew. I said, "Jesus, okay." That was it; that was my whole prayer.

Maybe a theologian would say that's not a prayer. But I couldn't pray anything florid, like, "O, compassionate Father who dwelleth in the highest heavenlies betwixt the cherubim...." I couldn't do that. Not that there's anything wrong with elegant words. God created them. God is the Word. But He looks at the true expression of your heart. He couldn't care less about fancy words.

As soon as I prayed those two words, everything was open. God looked right through me and saw that I meant, *I surrender.* Surrender is all-important. It's different from saying religious words. I used to be the most religious sinner on earth. I would get stoned and start witnessing to people about Jesus. Every time I passed a phone booth with the sinner's prayer plastered on the door, I would pray it. But that was not surrender. It's not enough to grow up knowing God is real, seeing miracles, and knowing what God is capable of doing.

I thought I was enlightened, so I took that "enlightened" knowledge and decided there must be another way to get to God.

It's the truth: Jesus is the *only* way to God. When I called out the name of Jesus by saying, "Jesus, okay," God knew what I meant. In those two little words, I was saying, "I repent. Forgive me! Heal me. Love me. I'm open. I'm ready to give it all to You this time; I'm not just muttering a prayer. I believe in You; I want You; I need You."

The power of God poured through me like fire. It burned through my mind and body. It burned through every part of my body and into my heart, into the deepest parts of my being. Everywhere that fire burned, it healed, restored, and strengthened. That fire was resurrection life.

Fire is the best word I could come up with to describe what I experienced. I've tried to compare it to hot or boiling honey because it was so sweet. The burning was as real as if I had stuck my hand into the flame of a candle or a fireplace, yet it didn't hurt. I was burning but I wasn't consumed, just like the burning bush Moses saw. This fire was burning through me. I was in a state of wonder.

The thing that amazed me the most wasn't that my mind or body was being healed, or that I was being released from so many addictions. That's not what amazed me the most. What amazed me the most was that Jesus loved me and had come to me. He was revealing Himself to me. I didn't know it could be for *me*.

In my heart, I could see Jesus being beaten, His beard torn, and His face spit on. I didn't think of this in a religious way, like the crucifixion paintings. I saw the actual, historic, brutal Roman torture, with Jesus so badly beaten. His face and body were so shredded and disfigured that you couldn't even recognize Him.

I saw the whip thrashing His back, over and over again for my healing. I saw Him being nailed to that cross, His blood flowing, the spear plunging into His side. At that point, I realized that Jesus suffered for me so I could be His. Did I understand it all right then? No, I couldn't understand it with my mind. I understand it more now, but at that time, I knew in my heart that He was whipped so I could be healed. In my deepest heart, I knew He shed His blood so I could be saved. I realized that He volunteered to be separated from the presence of God so I could be included, that He was bound so I could be free, and that He took my sicknesses and diseases so I could be healed.

I raised my hands and worshipped Him, right where I was. I wept; I just cried and cried. I actually raised my hands so I could worship the Lord. Even though I had grown up in church, I had always refused to raise my hands. I never raised my hands when everyone else did. I grew up in a Pentecostal church where big women would scream and throw their big hair. They scared me half to death. I usually bit my fingernails and stared out the window. If they told me to raise my hands, I stuck them in my pockets. But now I raised my hands. Now I knew what it was all about. I knew Jesus loved me, and I wept and wept.

I raised my fist over my head. All over the world, a raised fist symbolizes revolution. I didn't think about that at the time. I raised my fist and shouted, "I am free!" Talk about a revolution!

The devil had been defeated. It's the most complete revolution anyone can ever experience. The devil had been dethroned and Jesus had become my Lord! Hallelujah! I declared out loud, "I am free. I am free! Satan, you lost your slave. Tommy Ray O'Dell will never be your slave again!"

Nothing Was Ever the Same Again

When I was in Kenya, I met Peter Amakanji. Peter had been a crippled beggar for thirty years until he was healed in my grandfather's crusade in Nakuru in 1978. He witnessed to me and tried to reason with me before I surrendered my life to Jesus, but to no avail. Later, when he found out that I had gotten saved, he wrote to my grandfather and said he never thought I could be saved. He thought there was no hope for me, because I was so bad. When someone who has experienced God's miracle-working power himself gives up on you—*you know you're bad!*

Things that are impossible for people to imagine are possible with God. The Bible says that when your family gives up on you, God will pick you up. He will not forsake you. People told my parents to find me, knock me over the head, and lock me up in a psych ward where they could tranquilize me and I could live like a vegetable the rest of my life. That was the best they could offer. You see, when everybody gives up on you and the doctors, clinics, and psychologists say there is no hope—there is still hope with Jesus. That's not just a slogan on a bumper sticker. It's true! It's real, because *He* is real! This Gospel we preach is not a fairy tale.

I don't go into detail about sin when I give my testimony, because I don't want to glorify the devil. In fact, even though my life was a wreck and the devil seemed to have me under his control, I was not very impressed with his power. I have travelled around the globe and have journeyed to the witchcraft capitals of the world in West Africa, Brazil, and other parts of South America. I've seen what the devil has done and is still trying to do, yet none of it electrifies me like the power of Jesus. The power of the Living God makes an *impact!*

I had a fire in my heart to go back to Africa right after I met Jesus in May, 1981. I tried my best to get back, but I didn't have any money. Nobody would buy me a ticket. I was sixteen years old, with long hair and big moccasins. I didn't understand why no one would give me any money. They said, "You've got to do this and that and the other. You've got to settle down. You have a fire, but you need to wait and let your fire get mature."

I said, "Hey man, the only mature fire I know is ashes." So I left Tulsa. The Lord led me to different places. I went to Holland first, which is where I met my beautiful wife, Elisabeth. I learned to preach in the red light district of Amsterdam, Holland, where drugs are legal (this I did without doing drugs). That was my Bible school.

I preached to the junkies and prostitutes, as well as the needy and hurting people. The Dutch preachers liked my preaching, so some of them even let me preach in their churches. Even though I was young, I was excited. I had faith to believe God for miracles.

However, the people in the church did not like me preaching to the prostitutes and junkies. They didn't want *those* kinds of people in their church. So they had a meeting and called me out on the carpet. They said, "We don't want you going to those kinds of places anymore. We don't want you to go to the junkies or the heroin addicts or the homeless; we don't want you to go to the punkers, the lesbians, or the homosexuals. We don't want you to go to the people on the streets."

"Why not?" I asked.

One of the old preachers retorted, "If you go to Sodom, you become a Sodomite."

I was a little brash, but I said, "Do you know what the difference is between me and you preachers?" (Now, I know that's a bad start. I'm older and wiser now.) I said, "The difference between me and you is that I believe that what's on the inside of me is stronger than what's on the inside of them, and you don't! The rest of the world is not like America. It's dark. Other countries don't have a church on every street corner. Did you know that 92 percent of all the preachers in the world preach in America? People in Amsterdam don't have as much to choose from. So I am trying to do the best I can to work with everybody."

I wasn't trying to be cocky or arrogant. I was just telling them what I believed, because the Bible says that greater is He that is in me than He that is in the world (see 1 John 4:4). When I went to the frontlines, I didn't believe those devils were going to jump on me and stuff me full of witchcraft. I believed they were afraid of me and were looking for another part of town to run to.

The preacher said, "The devil is after you."

I responded, "No. I'm after him."

By now, the preacher was mad and said, "I will see you fall."

"Well," I said, "don't hold your breath, because you might be in for a long wait."

I knew that these Dutch Christians had heard about a girl in the Philippines who supposedly had been bitten by the devil, but they took it all wrong and got "spooky" about it. They were afraid of being bitten by devils, so I boldly declared, "No, I'm not afraid of being bitten by devils. I'll bite *them* instead!"

Then a beautiful young Dutch girl, who later became my wife, spoke up and said, "You shouldn't say that to the devil; he might get mad." All I could say was, "If I'm not making the devil mad, then what good am I doing in this world?" To my knowledge, there's nothing in the Bible about fearing the devil, giving him credit, or honoring him in any way.

After this, I had to leave the Netherlands. So I went to other countries, traveling and preaching. I went to Ireland, France, and Belgium. Most of the time, I went to the needy places and ministered to people on the streets because the churches wouldn't take me. Sometimes when I preached, I lived out in the woods. When I was eighteen years old, I had to register for the draft, but I didn't have an address because I was living in a tent in the woods of Northern Ireland. I wrote "cave hill outside of Belfast" as my address when I filled out the draft form.

The first two years were rough. I didn't have any support. People talk about living by faith, but I really *experienced* living by faith. During this time I got married. Can you imagine being dumb enough to get married, living like that? Elisabeth was naive enough to marry me. She didn't marry me for my looks, because my hair was long enough to cover my face. Sometimes all you could see was my nose. But everywhere we went, we preached Jesus and people got healed. We prayed for people to get filled with the Holy Ghost, and they did.

The only reason I even went to Europe was because I looked on a globe and noticed that Holland is closer to Africa than Tulsa. I am so glad I went to Holland or I would never have met my fabulous wife. Today we have five children and three grandchildren and have never been more in love.

Living in the Book of Acts Today

My grandparents, T.L. and Daisy Osborn, saw the anointing of God on my evangelistic efforts so they took Elisabeth and me under their experienced wings. They schooled us on how to be effective witnesses for Christ, regardless of what country we might be in or what cultural opposition we might face.

We conducted our first outreach campaigns in Central America. In Costa Rica and Honduras we saw blind eyes open, cripples walk, and deaf ears unstop. Thousands got saved. It was powerful!

We held our first mass campaign in Ghana in September, 1983. Twenty thousand people gathered to hear us in a field in Nkawkaw. We saw seventeen people healed of blindness. Nearly sixty people who had been deaf mutes from birth were healed. Every night, people who had been tormented by demons or involved in witchcraft were completely set free. Tens of thousands received Jesus. This was our beginning.

Later, we preached the Gospel all over Africa. We have travelled all around the world, preaching before millions of people in more than eighty nations for thirty-one years. In one of our most recent crusades in India, the crowds were estimated to be as large as 150,000 people nightly in a city called Dindigal. They had never seen anything like this before. We reached out to hundreds of unreached villages all around that city.

I want to be clear about something: The reason my wife and I have seen millions come to Jesus all over the world is not because I am some special saint. One reason that we have been so successful is because we were willing to venture to places where others wouldn't go. We have journeyed to dangerous, harsh places with unthinkable living conditions—real hell-holes. We buried a baby in Ghana. In another tropical country, my wife almost died of malaria. We have been stoned, threatened and arrested. One time in India, we were charged with a crime for practicing medicine without a license, but the case was thrown out. Another time, we showed up in New Guinea for a crusade in the middle of a tribal war. We felt like we were living in the book of Acts.

We have gone into such remote areas that if we died, nobody would have known about it for weeks. When you go into such neglected locales, you can be neglected. When you go to the forgotten, you can be forgotten also. But in spite of everything, we are still alive and going strong. In fact, we have seen more miracles in one day than most preachers will witness in a lifetime.

We continue to travel and preach, going places where few have gone before—to the urban centers, to the jungles, to the remote villages of forgotten people. Our mission is to proclaim the Gospel to ears that have yet to hear. Our goal is to display the healing power of God to eyes that have yet to see. Our ministry is called Frontier Evangelism because we direct our efforts toward the frontiers of civilization. With only faith and a translator to assist me, I have forded rivers, climbed mountains, and slashed through thick underbrush to reach those who have yet to hear the name of Jesus.

Once we blaze evangelistic trails to reach remote places, the Spirit of God touches hard-to-reach cultures with the Gospel message. Then we establish a base of operation and plant new churches for the new believers. During our first twelve years, Frontier Evangelism founded over fifty churches, each with their own native pastor. As of this writing, Frontier Evangelism has helped build and establish nearly three hundred churches in some of the most notoriously dangerous nations all over the world.

We have seen the forgotten. We have seen their hunger. When we acknowledge their presence and take up our cross and preach Jesus to their hearts, we can prove the truth of the Gospel message with the evidence of signs and wonders. This driving purpose to tell others about Jesus is an unquenchable fire within us.

We conducted more than seventy crusades in twenty-five nations in our first ten years of ministry. Our audiences ranged from the Hindus of India to the Juju practitioners of Africa. Since then, our message has been heard by millions of Muslims, animists, European atheists, South American Roman Catholics, and Protestants of Northern Ireland. In each of our overseas meetings, 30,000 to 150,000 people thronged the platform in response to positive words of hope and healing. Always, before astonished eyes, the crippled walk, the deaf hear, the blind see, and those who have diseases are instantly and miraculously healed.

We have traveled to eighty different countries, preaching at hundreds of crusades, conferences, refugee camps, and prison outreaches. Our message includes the message of Isaiah: "Strengthen ye the weak hands, and confirm the feeble knees. Say to them that are of a fearful heart, Be strong, fear not: behold, your God will come with vengeance, even God with a recompence; he will come and save you. Then the eyes of the blind shall be opened, and the ears of the deaf shall be unstopped. Then shall the lame man leap as an hart, and the tongue of the dumb sing: for in the wilderness shall waters break out, and streams in the desert" (Isaiah 35:3–6, KJV).

Notice that it says, "God will come with a recompence. He will come and save you." Recompense is revenge. God will come with vengeance, but the vengeance is not directed against the people who need Him. It is directed against our enemy, Satan, and it works on our behalf.

Chapter 2

What Is Faith?

Don't you believe that I am in the Father, and that the Father is in me? The words I say to you I do not speak on my own authority. Rather, it is the Father, living in me, who is doing his work. Believe me when I say that I am in the Father and the Father is in me; or at least believe on the evidence of the works themselves. Very truly I tell you, whoever believes in me will do what I have been doing, and they will do even greater things than these, because I am going to the Father. And I will do whatever you ask in my name, so that the Father may be glorified in the Son. You may ask me for anything in my name, and I will do it.

(John 14:10–14, NIV)

These words of Jesus are powerful spiritual seeds that will produce real spiritual fruit in us when they are nurtured by the Holy Spirit. The Bible is a miracle book, filled with stories of supernatural events. If we removed all references to God's miracles from the Bible, we would have a much thinner Bible and the main themes of faith would become meaningless.

God's miracle life is the same today as it was during Bible days. I believe God is as eager to display His awesome power today as He was in the days of the apostle Paul. God is still causing cripples to rise and walk, deaf ears to hear, blind eyes to see, and all types of incurable diseases to be healed. The Book of Acts, also known as the Acts of the Apostles or the Acts of the Holy Spirit, continues to be written today. It's the one book from the Bible that never ends.

The book of Acts continues to unfold in and through the lives of modern believers all around the world, because the Holy Ghost is still "acting." Every time we write about the things that happen in one of our mass miracle campaigns, it's like a new chapter in the Book of Acts. Likewise, every time God does something wonderful in your life, it is a continuation of the Book of Acts. Marvelous new chapters are being written daily. Nothing can stop this book from growing and expanding throughout the earth. Every time you open your eyes and exercise your faith, you are living in the Book of Acts. This is exciting!

In fact, some very powerful teachers, soul-winners, evangelists, and pastors may be reading these words. Some great champions of the faith will be able to step forward by putting these biblical truths into action. This faith message could be for you.

What Is Faith?

There are many definitions for *faith*, but the most profound is deceptively simple: Faith in God is trusting in His love, as the leper trusted. "When Jesus came down from the mountainside, large crowds followed him. A man with leprosy came and knelt before him and said, 'Lord if you are willing, you can make me clean.' Jesus reached out his hand and touched the man. 'I am willing,' he said. 'Be clean!' Immediately he was cleansed of his leprosy" (Matthew 8:1–3, NIV).

What is faith? Faith is the secret door through which we enter into the realm of the supernatural. We discover the highest level of faith simply by believing in God's love. There is a story in the gospels of Matthew, Mark, and Luke about a man afflicted with leprosy who came to Jesus for healing. That simple leper man asked a question that many great thinkers, theologians, philosophers and kings have tried to ask. He knelt before Jesus and said, "Lord, I know You can heal me—if You will." And this is the question: What is the will of God? Most people don't know what the will of God is. Even many Christians don't really know. It is murky to them, an impenetrable mystery. So how can you find God's will?

"Jesus answered: 'Don't you know me, Philip, even after I have been among you such a long time? Anyone who has seen me has seen the Father" (John 14:9 NIV). "The one who sent me is with me; he has not left me alone, for I always do what pleases him" (John 8:29 NIV). Jesus revealed God's essence. He showed the world what God is like. He showed us a perfect portrait of the Father's will, love, and character, not only through His words, but through His actions also.

With Jesus as our great example, we can answer the question, "What is God's will?" God's will is reflected in His nature. His will is the same as His character and temperament as demonstrated by His Son, Jesus. Since you cannot trust what you do not know, you have to understand who God is in order to believe in Him intelligently.

God Is Love

Faith in God means trusting in His love. Here is how Jesus said it:

"Dear friends, let us love one another, for love comes from God. Everyone who loves has been born of God and knows God. Whoever does not love does not know God, because **God is love.** *This is how God showed his love among us: He sent his one and only Son into the world that we might live through him. This is love: not that we loved God, but that he loved us and sent his Son as an atoning sacrifice for our sins. Dear friends, since God so loved us, we also ought to love one another. No one has ever seen God; but if we love one another, God lives in us and his love is made complete in us.... And so we know and rely on the love God has for us.* **God is love.** *Whoever lives in love lives in God, and God in them. This is how love is made complete among us so that we will have confidence on the day of judgment: In this world we are like Jesus. There is no fear in love. But perfect love drives out fear, because fear has to*

do with punishment. The one who fears is not made perfect in love" (1 John 4:7–12; 16–18, NIV, emphasis mine).

Twice in the same chapter John declares, "God is love." Love is what God is. Understanding His love and believing it—this is the great secret that unlocks faith. You can only believe in someone to the extent that you have confidence in that person's good will toward you. If you consider me and become convinced that I am a man of love, it will not be hard to trust my promises to you. If you think that I have your best interest at heart, it is easy to believe what I say. If you believe that I love you, it will be natural to believe me when I give my word to you. If I guarantee something, you tend to believe me because, quite simply, you understand my will and know that I carry good will toward you.

The leper was asking Jesus, "I know You have the *ability* to cleanse me, but do You have the *desire* to do it?" He already knew that God was able to heal him, but he didn't know Jesus well enough to be convinced of His willingness to do so. He was confused about God's will in the matter.

Jesus answered his question forcefully and once and for all. "Jesus was indignant, He reached out his hand and touched the man. 'I am willing,' he said. 'Be clean!' Immediately the leprosy left him and he was cleansed" (Mark 1:41–42, NIV). In the same way, when you or I are filled with God's compassion, the power of God will begin to flow through us. All of God's power is "love power."

When a person is filled with compassion, he immediately begins to be moved with compassion as well. Faith without actions is dead! (See James 2:14–22.) The same is true about love. Love without actions is dead. You cannot love someone if you don't act in love.

My grandfather once told a story about a wise preacher. This wise preacher saw a group of Christians who got together every week for all-night prayer. He listened to their prayers. They prayed for the lost to be saved. They prayed for the backslidden to come back to church. They also prayed for certain people who were notorious sinners.

After the all-night prayer meeting, the preacher gathered them together and told them, "You prayed for the lost to be found, you prayed for the backslidden to come back to church, and you prayed for some people by name to be saved and come to Jesus. But they will never be reached as long as you merely just pray. You must let the love of Jesus shine through your eyes. Allow Him to reach out and touch them through your hands. Your love is only in word. You must unite your prayers with deeds. Jesus told us: Go ye into all the world and preach the Gospel to every creature. You've got to go tell them about God's grace and love. Then you will be showing love in action."

Yes, we must pray, but afterward we should go out and preach and do the works of God. That is the will of God. In all of our meetings, large or small, we want the works of God to demonstrate His love and bring people to faith in God as their Savior.

A Young Man Healed: Seth

Here is a story of a wonderful miracle that took place on the second day of one of our crusades. The crowd was eager to receive from God as they saw God's power mightily demonstrated the previous night. A young man named Seth was in particular need of a demonstration of God's love. For fifteen years, Seth had a large running sore on his leg. The festering hole had resisted all treatment and would not heal on its own. He had been to many hospitals and clinics without any success. He needed a miracle!

As Seth listened to the Good News being preached from the rugged platform, his faith began to grow. When it was time for the prayer of healing, Seth was ready. He laid his hand on his wound and believed God. When the prayer was finished, he took his hand away and to his amazement, he saw that the open sore had closed and was perfectly healed. As he testified on the platform, we checked his leg. The place on his leg where the sore had been looked like a large scar that had been healed for years. That is the power of God's compassion and love activated through faith!

Helping Each Other Reach for His Hand

One chapter before the "God is love" passage quoted above, we read: "This is how we know what love is: Jesus Christ laid down his life for us. And we ought to lay down our lives for our brothers and sisters. If anyone has material possessions and sees a brother or sister in need but has no pity on them, how can the love of

God be in that person? Dear children, let us not love with words or speech but with actions and in truth. This is how we know that we belong to the truth and how we set our hearts at rest in his presence: If our hearts condemn us, we know that God is greater than our hearts, and he knows everything. Dear friends, if our hearts do not condemn us, we have confidence before God and receive from him anything we ask, because we keep his commands and do what pleases him. And this is his command: to believe in the name of his Son, Jesus Christ, and to love one another as he commanded us. The one who keeps God's commands lives in him, and he in them. And this is how we know that he lives in us: We know it by the Spirit he gave us (1 John 3:16-24, NIV).

By the Spirit He has given to us, we know our heavenly Father. We are motivated by His love. Faith in God means believing in His amazing love. When we believe in His love, we act in love ourselves. Trusting His promises becomes easy. Faith is no longer a mystery, because we know and trust God's character, which has been revealed in Jesus. Our faith is the natural result of knowing God's nature. Acting in faith is not complicated at all once the revelation of the light of our Father's goodness bursts through our darkness.

Seth's story reminds me of a wonderful miracle that happened in one of our meetings in Ghana, West Africa. There was a poor village woman who had only one son. Several years before, a mysterious sore that refused to heal surfaced on his left leg. Before long, he was diagnosed with leprosy. The leprosy slowly spread, eating its way inexorably through skin, into muscles and even penetrating the nerves of both of his legs. By the time he reached the age of twelve, his legs had become paralyzed.

The woman was too poor to afford the expensive treatments in the capital city, Accra, so she just did her best, bandaging the oozing wounds and carrying her son wherever he needed to go. One day, her neighbor came to her hut and told her of the miracle campaign that I was preaching in Sunyani, thirty kilometers away. She had nothing to lose, so she wrapped her son on her back, binding him with her *kanga* and began the arduous trek through the forest.

As she forded streams and maneuvered over the rough bush trails, she rehearsed in her mind what she would do when she found me in Sunyani. She was not a believer, so she assumed that I was a traditional healer or a witch doctor. She had brought all the money she possessed, expecting to meet me privately and offer her payment. She thought she would pay me so I would spill chicken's blood, mutter incantations, or do whatever an *obruni* (foreigner) who practiced the healing arts might do to cure her son.

At last, she arrived. It was already dark and she felt exhausted after her long journey. The driver of a gaudily painted *tro tro* (cheap taxi truck that hauls loads of passengers squashed together for maximum profit), directed her to the large open field where I was preaching every night and praying for the sick. Imagine how her heart broke when she realized that far from getting a personal audience with the *obruni* witch doctor, she couldn't even get near the platform where I stood preparing to preach. The crowd had swelled to nearly thirty thousand, as more and more people continued to inundate the field. Many lame, blind, deaf, and insane people were being carried or led in.

This woman struggled to get as close as she could, but her tired body finally gave out. With tears, she undid her *kanga* and allowed her son to crumple to the ground. She gazed up toward the platform where I was standing, unable to disguise her disappointment that her venture was not going the way she had anticipated. As she felt the eagerness and excitement of the multitude, she became curious and began to listen to my sermon. She wondered how my preaching was going to deal with all these needy people.

I preached the wonderful, everlasting Gospel of Jesus the Messiah. I told stories about the life of Jesus and commenced with the one about the leper being healed. This woman had never heard anything like this before. She listened in amazement as I told story after story of healing miracles from the Bible. She reasoned that this Messiah could definitely do anything, but she privately wondered about His willingness to help her son.

As I reached the end of my sermon, I related how Jesus died on the cross, emphasizing the love He carried for us—enough love to cause Him to suffer and die so we could be free. The story of the cross is the greatest love story that has ever been told. In graphic detail, I described how Jesus was humiliated and tortured—His back flayed open, the cruel nails, and the unendurable pain. I proclaimed, "He suffered so you could be healed! He died so you could be resurrected! He was cursed so you could be blessed! He descended to hell so you could enter heaven! Jesus loves you and wants to save and heal you. The cross *proves* His love!"

At that moment, both the woman and her young son believed in the love of Jesus, the Messiah. Weeping, they prayed, along with tens of thousands of others on that field to welcome new life into their hearts. They knew that He loved them and their sins were forgiven.

I began to pray for the healing of those who had come with various diseases. Still unable to draw any closer to the platform, this dedicated mother reverently laid her work-leathered hands on her son's lifeless legs. Suddenly, a healing fire swept into his body, penetrating skin, muscle, nerve and bone. Then she and the people around her tore the oozing, crusted rags from his legs. Underneath the bandages, his formerly leprous skin had become fresh and healthy!

The mother grabbed her son by the hand, hauling him to his feet, as she shouted, "Boy, I have carried you far enough!" He rose and began to walk, jump, and rejoice. After he pressed himself through the crowd to the platform, he began to run back and forth in front of the crowd. The entire crowd exploded with praise and exclamations of joy!

Chapter 3

What Is Ministry?

My grandfather, T.L. Osborn, taught me a simple but powerful truth: "God," he said, "gives you two things. First, He gives you salvation, and then He gives you a ministry." In other words, everyone who has received Jesus as Messiah is a minister. This includes you as well as me. You may not be a platform preacher but if you believe the Gospel message, you can declare, "I am an ambassador of the highest Kingdom! I am friends with Jesus! Everything Jesus did to me, He wants to do through me! Christ is in me, the hope of glory. Jesus loves through me. He heals through me. He saves through me. I am His witness. I am on His team. Together we are unbeatable!"

Do you believe that? If you have trouble believing this, consider the Gerasene demoniac, who was one of the most unlikely ministers you can think of. Here is his story from the Bible:

> *"They went across the lake to the region of the Gerasenes. When Jesus got out of the boat, a man with an impure spirit came from the tombs to meet him. This man lived in the tombs, and no one could bind him anymore, not even with a chain.*

For he had often been chained hand and foot, but he tore the chains apart and broke the irons on his feet. No one was strong enough to subdue him. Night and day among the tombs and in the hills he would cry out and cut himself with stones.

When he saw Jesus from a distance, he ran and fell on his knees in front of him. He shouted at the top of his voice, 'What do you want with me, Jesus, Son of the Most High God? In God's name don't torture me!' For Jesus had said to him, 'Come out of this man, you evil spirit!'

Then Jesus asked him, 'What is your name?'

'My name is Legion,' he replied, 'for we are many.' And he begged Jesus again and again not to send them out of the area.

A large herd of pigs was feeding on the nearby hillside. The demons begged Jesus, 'Send us among the pigs; allow us to go into them.' He gave them permission, and the impure spirits came out and went into the pigs. The herd, about two thousand in number, rushed down the steep bank into the lake and were drowned.

Those tending the pigs ran off and reported this in the town and countryside, and the people went out to see what had happened. When they came to Jesus, they saw the man who had been possessed by the legion of demons, sitting there, dressed and in his right mind; and they were afraid. Those who had seen it told the people what had happened to the demon-possessed man—and told about the pigs as well. Then the people began to plead with Jesus to leave their region.

As Jesus was getting into the boat, the man who had been demon-possessed begged to go with him. Jesus did not let him, but said, 'Go home to your own people and tell them how much the Lord has done for you, and how he has had mercy on you.' So the man went away and began to tell in the Decapolis how much Jesus had done for him. And all the people were amazed" *(Mark 5:1–20, NIV).*

This man was possessed with more than a thousand demonic personalities and has led a weird, tormented life, dwelling naked among the tombs of the dead, slicing himself until he bled profusely, and groaning aloud in his self-inflicted torture. He was a horrifying figure. Many times the people had sought to capture and restrain him, but he always snapped the chains like string. Yet during his first encounter with Jesus, this unapproachable demoniac crumpled at His feet.

The power of Jesus is far greater than the power of demons. Jesus simply commanded the demons to depart. They bargained with Him saying, "Let us go into the pigs." Jesus allowed them to depart from the man and enter into the pigs. The moment they did, the pigs tore over the cliff and plunged to their death. Instantly, the man was completely healed of the madness that had made him act like a beast for so long.

When the citizens of the town came running and found the man clean, clothed, and in his right mind, they were amazed. But instead of being elated that something wonderful and supernatural had taken place, they were furious. They were afraid because the pigs were their livelihood. They became absurdly obsessed with the loss of the pigs. Pigs, which were unclean animals to the Jews, were a source of great income during this time because their owners could sell their meat to the Romans for quite a profit. They missed the miracle because they were only thinking about money.

They begged Jesus to leave. Jesus left without argument and proceeded to get into the boat with His disciples. But the man who had been liberated from demons held onto Him and pleaded, "Don't go! I want to be with You, I want to be on Your team. Don't leave me here with them." Jesus insisted that staying there would be the best thing, and told him to go to his family and tell them how God had been compassionate to him. So the man did. He told his family about the miracle—but he didn't stop there. He preached his testimony in all ten towns of Decapolis. Everywhere he went, people were amazed with his story. When Jesus came through the region on His return trip, everyone received Him because of that one man's ministry!

What God Does to You,
He Wants to do Through You

This story shows us the meaning of ministry. It proves that what God does to you, He wants to do through you. Never forget that. You have a ministry because you have a story of God's love that the world needs to hear. That's what ministry is all about. Has

He healed you? If so, then you are qualified to be an instrument of healing. Has He saved you? If so, then you are qualified to be a conduit of salvation. Has He set you free? Has He blessed you? Has He transformed you? If so, then let Him do the same through you. Jesus said, "Freely you have received, freely give" (Matthew 10:8, NKJV).

We need a source and an outlet. A stream that has an inflow but no outflow of water will become unwholesome, stagnant, and a breeding place for disease. Likewise, if we only receive God's love but never give it out, we cannot stay pure. In order to remain uncontaminated, we need to allow God's love to flow into our spirits, and then flow out to the world!

An Anointed Ministry

If we are uncertain about our calling and ministry, then we cannot be effective in this. God's anointing gives us the confidence and ability we need. We hear the term "the anointing" a lot. We tend to think of "the anointing" as a mysterious power that only works through certain, very special individuals. But that's not true.

In the Old Testament, prophets, kings, Levites and high priests were the only ones anointed to serve in special offices. The term "Anointed One," or "Messiah" (in Greek, "the Christ") refers to the One who would come as King, Priest and sacrificial lamb. But now that the Anointed One, Jesus, has borne our sins as our substitute, we have access to the same Spirit that raised Him from the dead. Today all believers can be anointed with God's supernatural energy and life.

The word *anointing* does not indicate something that is out of reach. *Anointing* simply means an appointment, a job, a task, or a commission. That's how the word is commonly used in the Bible. An anointing is always accompanied with the ability to fulfill that specific job. When God anoints us, He shows us He has chosen us for an assignment and that He will supply the supernatural energy needed to complete our particular tasks.

Sometimes people kneel down before great men or women of God (they've even done this to me), and beg for some of their anointing. This reveals that they do not know how God operates. I cannot deliver a portion of my anointing to you, however I can pray for you to receive the baptism in the Holy Spirit. Then if you believe, you will be anointed with power from God's supernatural realm. Your anointing may not be identical to mine, but it can be just as powerful.

The Bible teaches us to pray for the sick by laying our hands on them as we pray. It is also appropriate to lay hands on people in order to transfer the baptism of the Holy Spirit and other blessings to them. However, it is unscriptural to believe that a human being can decide what particular gifts to possess or transfer to others. "For it is God which worketh in you both to will and to do of his good pleasure" (Philippians 2:13, KJV).

When many believers speak of "the anointing," they are not talking about being filled with the Spirit. They are referring to specific gifts of the Spirit. The baptism of the Spirit is the fountainhead through which all the special gifts flow. We receive God's anointing primarily for the purpose of being a convincing witness of Jesus' resurrection through our speech, gifts of healing, and other manifestations of the Spirit. The apostle Paul explained it this way, "I wish that all of you were as I am. But each of you has your own gift from God; one has this gift, another has that" (1 Corinthians 7:7, NIV).

I like to pray for people to receive Jesus, the source of all power and gifts, but I cannot determine what specific job God has for them. God has a job for each one of us and He will always give us the power and resources required to fulfill our profession. Remember, all the particular parts of the body of Christ work together for the single purpose of rescuing people from Satan's clutch and bringing them into God's family. Every believer has a marvelous role to play in fulfilling God's grand destiny.

God gives us the desire to fulfill a specific calling or duty and then mightily equips us to fulfill it. In other words, He gives us the passion to do His will and then matches that passion with the ability to achieve His perfect goal. When we receive the Holy Spirit, we tap into the limitless potential of God's resurrection life. We no longer merely dwell in the natural realm; we are translated into the supernatural sphere.

The way to demonstrate God's power is by receiving the Spirit of God and then discovering our part in His amazing plan. Once we discover who we are, we must hold fast to that revelation.

Sometimes I simply say, "Find a self and stick with it." Remember, God's highest purpose is always love. All of His power is love power.

Called and Equipped

An anointing does not equip us to be instantly skillful as God's minister. Growing in an anointing takes a lot of practice. When we first get saved and receive the Holy Spirit, we are excited, yet not capable of doing very much. The only way to become more effective is by practicing. It's true—we grow by giving; we learn how to help others by doing; we learn how to reach people by using what we've got; we learn how to heal the sick by exercising our faith in love.

All believers must use what they've got. Just like a musician needs to hone his craft, God has promised us that if we apply our gifts, He will be faithful to multiply more into our lives. "Whoever has will be given more, and they will have an abundance. Whoever does not have, even what they have will be taken from them" (Matthew 13:12, NIV). Those who are good stewards of the investment their heavenly Father has so generously bestowed on them will enjoy an unending supply of His resurrection power!

Spiritual practice is a lot like physical exercise. We know what it feels like to exercise regularly and to feel and see our muscles grow in size and strength. The muscles already present in our body are part of God's creative gift, but the task of caring for those muscles is up to us. If we just lie down and do nothing, our muscles will atrophy in just a few weeks. We will become nearly crippled and have to relearn how to use our muscles in our legs in order to walk again. Likewise, when we exercise our spiritual muscles, the anointing becomes more effective and powerful.

This is another reason that we cannot simply request someone else's anointing. When people come and kneel down, asking a famous preacher for his anointing, does it work? Do they get up and start bringing people to faith through their magnificent preaching? No! It takes a lot of work to become proficient in the art of winning souls. When God anoints us, we have to add action to the anointing, just like we add action to faith and love.

Imagine a masterful piano player who has been playing his instrument for over forty years. He can play any style of music: classical, jazz, blues, gospel. You name it; he can play it! Now imagine a young person watching him and thinking, *Oh! He is wonderful. I want to play like him more than anything. I need to. I want that gift. I must play like that. Give me that gift. I want it so bad.* In desperation, the young person falls in front of the old master musician, begging him to transfer his ability, talent, and years of blood, sweat, and tears, along with all of his life experiences—the pain and triumphs that flowed through his fingers into that piano. He exclaims, "Just touch me and I'll play like you!"

Would that work? No, absolutely not! I can imagine the old man gently lifting the young "would-be" musician to his feet and telling him kindly, "My son, God has already given you the passion, desire and love for music. He has blessed you with a musical ear and rhythm. Those are the supreme gifts a musician needs. Now the rest is up to you. You must study, practice, perform, and live; your music will grow as your soul grows."

That piano player's gift came from God, yet he had to practice. The Father of Lights has given us all gifts and talents, but there is no quick and easy way to become a master of our craft. It takes effort. It takes prayer. It takes study. It takes fasting. And most of all, it takes practice.

Practice in the world where people are lost and lonely—in jails and prisons, the marketplace, and on the streets. We can journey to the villages of the mission fields where billions of desperate souls truly need Jesus. Practice your anointing! Allow the water of Life to flow through you. Give out of what you have received and you will stay pure. That is a lifestyle that can change your world. You don't have to be like me or anyone else. Be the best that you can be!

Treasures from the Storehouse

How would you like to see real miracles in your ministry? Every believer can experience the miracle life. I want to teach you some of the secrets the Holy Spirit has taught me. I want to open my heart and expose the treasures that will launch you into a supernatural life of miracles and wonders. I want your ministry to be enhanced with more splendor than you ever dreamed possible. I see miracles every week, and you will see miracles too, if you understand these foundational truths.

Healing is for everyone. We are children of an awe-inspiring covenant and our redemptive blessings include healing. We can be healed ourselves and then we can freely give away to others what we have freely received.

How can you minister healing to the sick? Most people don't have a clue. First of all, you have to really identify with the covenant of healing: Jesus bore our sickness; He carried our pains and with His stripes we are healed (Isaiah 53:4-5; Matthew 8:17). This is a fact. I believe it. I have complete faith in this. Because of what Jesus said and did, I am sure about the will of God concerning healing. I know that it is part of my covenant that was paid for by the blood of Jesus. If you want to minister healing to others, you have to be sure about the source of healing in the first place. As long as you are unsure about God's covenant of healing, you cannot be used to bring healing to others.

Another foundational truth is that God wants to reach the whole world with the Gospel message (Mark 16:15). At Frontier Evangelism, we have dedicated most of our efforts to doing this. In particular, our Mission to the Unreached Peoples is an interdenominational effort that we have been taking very seriously for thirty years. Our passion is to assist the helpless among the world's least-reached peoples, and lead believers in church planting.

Why do we use the term, "unreached?" Who are the "unreached" peoples? The "unreached" are any people group among which there is no indigenous community of believing Christians with adequate numbers and resources to evangelize it. Geographically, most of the unreached people groups can be found within what is known as the 10/40 Window. This is the part of the world between the tenth and fortieth parallels of latitude above the equator. The 10/40 Window is like a belt around the globe. It covers much of northern and Saharan Africa and most of Asia. Some of the people are atheists, but most of them adhere to Muslim, Jewish, Hindu, Buddhist, or animist belief systems. They face many challenges, not the least of which is limited access to the Gospel message.

Whether I am preaching in the streets of Amsterdam or somewhere in India, I must know how to preach a message that works. For instance, let's say I have traveled to a city in West Africa and advertised with posters, newspaper, radio, banners, handbills, and a sound car. I have made every effort to advertise by using a combination of *rhema* and *logos*, the spoken and written word, because many of the people are illiterate and cannot read the posters.

All of the advertisements declare and reemphasize the promise that the blind will see, the deaf will hear, the cripples will walk, and the sick will be healed. The advertisement is powerful and compelling because we are saying that Jesus himself is going to show up at the campaign and the power of the Holy Spirit will be there. All of the churches are invited, regardless of denomination. If there are no churches, we will plant one.

The people respond to the invitation to come to the meeting. They throng the field, crowding around the platform—a sea of suffering and desperate humanity. What do I preach? What do I say to people with such incredible needs? There is only one message that God has promised to always confirm with miracles and that's the message of the Gospel, the Good News. As a result, every single time I preach I expect to see miracles of salvation, healing, and transformed lives. Under the anointing of God, I combine the Good News of spiritual salvation with the powerful evidence of healing and other miracles.

The greatest miracle of all is the eternal one. All other miracles are mere shadows of the most extreme miracle, the miracle of the new birth. I preach the birth of Jesus (a miracle birth), the life of Jesus (a miracle life), and the death and resurrection of Jesus (the greatest miracle of all). I preach the Gospel story of God's design for human beings. I talk about Satan's fraud, Christ's emancipation, and our reinstatement to fullness of life. I have found that if I preach that, God will confirm that message with miracles!

Another way to share the Good News is to simply tell a miracle story from the Bible, adding some Scriptures to reinforce the message.

> *"Bless the LORD, O my soul; And all that is within me, bless His holy name! Bless the LORD, O my soul, And forget not all His benefits: Who forgives all your iniquities, Who heals all your diseases, Who redeems your life from destruction, Who crowns you with lovingkindness and tender mercies" (Psalm 103:1–4, NKJV).*

"*By His stripes we are healed*" *(Isaiah 53:5, NKJV).*

"*As many as touched were made perfectly whole*" *(Matthew 14:36, KJV).*

"*Whosoever shall call upon the name of the* LORD *shall be saved*" *(Romans 10:13, KJV).*

After telling a miracle story from the Bible, I relate a modern-day miracle. It is imperative to master the art of storytelling in order to reach the unreached. All around the world, there is a universal fascination with a well-told story. Jesus taught people using parables, stories with a message. My stories come from my own life experiences.

A Witch in Argentina

I have experienced so many amazing miracles during my twenty-seven years of preaching—thousands of dramatic healings and many other supernatural events. So by now, I have a lot of stories. These stories swirl around in my head, and I call them "faith adventures."

Here is a story of a real-life witch in Argentina. The Bible promises that believers have power over all the power of the enemy. "Greater is he that is in you, than he that is in the world" (1 John 4:4 KJV). The following story highlights this theme.

In Tucumán, Argentina, I had a remarkable encounter with the powers of witchcraft and the occult. As I preached a healing and miracle outreach, I kept declaring to the people, "Jesus drank your cup, so you can drink His cup!" I was referring to Jesus, in the garden of Gethsemane, calling out to His Father: "If it is possible, let this cup pass from Me" (Matthew 26:39 NKJV). I told the crowd that Jesus drank our cup of poison and hate. He drank every drop of our condemnation and evil. He drained all of our curse and pain, so we might in turn drink His cup of freedom, healing, and righteousness.

Thousands of Argentines received Jesus. Hundreds were miraculously healed of everything from blindness and deafness to paralysis. However, one individual was not happy about all of these wonderful demonstrations of God's love. This particular woman had been a witch most of her life. She attended one of the services and afterward, with her mind cloaked in a demonic rage, she attempted to cast spells to kill me instantly. The evil forces within her were driving her to try to destroy me, or at least stop me from preaching about Satan's defeat.

The more she tried, the more she realized all of her witchcraft was powerless in harming me. Later, she said it was as if I was blanketed with a wall of radiant light and she couldn't pierce through it. She stormed out of the meeting in disgust. The evil spirits that controlled her were livid with impotent hatred.

She didn't give up though. I was having a private meeting with Pastor José when she burst into the office. Her face was a hideous mask of venomous spite. The moment she entered, the temperature in the room suddenly dropped and we shivered from the coldness, even though it was a scorching summer day in Tucumán. She grimaced horribly and then confessed that she had tried to kill me with demonic spells. Even though I was shivering, I remembered the Bible says, "Greater is he that is in you, than he that is in the world" (1 John 4:4, KJV).

When I think of this woman who was such a puppet of the enemy, I am reminded that everyone who refuses liberty in Christ is to one degree or another, a slave. People talk about the sinister genius of Satan, but how smart could he be? He tried to take on God.

I declared, "In the name of Jesus, I command you evil spirits to come out of her!" The woman became rigid as a board for several seconds and then she quietly collapsed to the ground. The temperature returned to normal again. When she opened her eyes, her whole expression was transformed. She began to weep with gratitude, sobbing uncontrollably and saying in Spanish, "*Soy libre, soy libre!* I'm free, I'm free!" Trembling with joy, she added, "If only I had known that I could be free, I would have come to Jesus years ago. I was afraid, so afraid. But now, I can tell that the evil spirits that have tormented me for all these years are gone." Immediately, I led her to the Lord in a simple salvation prayer and prayed for her to receive the baptism of the Holy Spirit. As she was inundated with the love and peace of God, the countenance of her face changed as it radiated with the love of heaven.

Jesus Christ, who is the same yesterday, today, and forever, saved her. God is love. His mercies endure forever. When you believe on the name of Jesus, you receive the authority of a believer. The Word becomes your sword; the Spirit becomes your power!

Chapter 4

The Key Ingredient

The simple steps we take when preaching to the unreached can be learned. I want to share the secrets that have made us victorious in over three decades of miracle evangelism. I want to open up a treasure trove of truth. These techniques can be learned and will enhance your ministry gift, but the faith that produces the supernatural evidence must be received as a gift from God. Understanding your authority as a believer is a revelation gift from the Holy Spirit.

After you receive this secret ingredient, you can hone your skill as a unique minister in God's service. We have already talked about what to preach. First, you tell a miracle story from the Bible (old miracle). Then, you tell a modern miracle story (new miracle). The third thing you need to do is encourage the people by saying, "Jesus will do the same miracles here for you." It is absolutely essential that you truly believe this. You have to mean what you say. You have to believe in the power of the Gospel. Don't say things you don't believe. If you can believe it, have courage to expect the supernatural result. Be bold!

Usually when I preach around the world I have an interpreter translate what I say, word for word, into the most common language of that particular region. Many times, my interpreter will perform splendidly throughout the whole service, but then turn to jelly at a crucial moment when I really need him to be brave, like when I'm praying for salvation or for the sick. Sometimes when I ask, "How many of you are healed right now? Raise your hand right now," the interpreter who was just roaring like a lion, becomes like a mouse—gesturing limply with a quivering voice. This is terrible!

Ideally, the interpreter should follow the inflection, tone, gestures, body language, and volume of the preacher. Why do these interpreters go limp at the most critical time? Their faith fails, that's why. Why does their faith fail? Because they don't have a revelation of God's love. Why don't they have a revelation of God's love? Because they don't have a revelation of what Jesus accomplished on the cross to purchase redemption. They have no personal revelation of the power of the living Jesus.

Faith is the secret ingredient. When my words are being interpreted, sometimes faith gets lost in the translation. If we preach the message of power, God will confirm it with demonstrative evidence. If we take authority over the spirits of infirmity and command them to leave in the name of Jesus, the Lord will never fail us. He will back us up and the powers of hell will be driven out. If we encourage the people to put their faith in Jesus into action, miracles will occur. Only the witness with evidence wins the case. We do not bring the world an empty religious message. We bring the world a living, healing, miracle Gospel!

Faith in Action

When it's time to pray for the sick after preaching, I take authority over all the satanic power of the enemy. I come against the spirits of sickness, blindness, deafness, paralysis, and all infirmities and plagues. I take authority over them, commanding them to go in the name of Jesus. I am confident that I have authority over them in the name of Jesus.

The name of Jesus is the name of authority and if I use that name, Satan must obey. If I use the name of Jesus one time, I know that is enough. I know the Gospel message works. It doesn't matter what I see at the moment. Remember the parable of the fig tree. Jesus commanded the fig tree to die, yet it still appeared to be alive. However, the next day as He and the disciples passed by, it was withered and dead (Matthew 21:18–22; Mark 11:12-14).

I preach the Gospel because it is the power of God to salvation for everyone who believes it (Romans 1:16). I have faith in the name of Jesus when I pray. I pray that God's healing power will flow through their bodies, opening blind eyes and deaf ears and taking away all manner of sickness and disease. But I don't stop there. I command in Jesus' name: "Blind eyes open! Deaf ears hear! Sickness be healed! Rise up and walk if you are lame!"

When you read the Bible, you will see that's the way Jesus healed. He didn't say long prayers; He used a word of command. That's when it happens. He said to blind Bartimaeus, "Receive your sight!" (Mark 10:46–52). He said to the man with the withered hand, "Stretch forth your hand!" (Matthew 12:10–13). He commanded the paralytic, "Rise up and take up your bed and walk!" (Matthew 9:2–6; Mark 2:3–12). That's powerful! Jesus didn't pray for the sick; He *commanded* them to be well. He didn't pray for the dead; He *commanded* them to rise: "Lazarus, come forth!" (John 11:43).

I fully believe that what I command will happen. I believe in God's love. God loves us and He's not going to let us down. God loves the lost and wants to help them. Jesus died on the cross to provide these blessings; you don't have to beg Him to do what He already longs to do. All you have to do is act in faith. It's not magic; it's authority.

The "anointing" is not some magical cloud. The anointing is our power; miracles are our job. The anointing will never leave us. Some preachers talk as if the anointing comes and goes, but I know that my anointing is always with me. Just as I never stop being who I am and you never stop being who you are, we never lose what God gives us. We just need to learn how to use the anointing more effectively.

After I preach, pray and command—I rejoice. The Bible says, "Whatever things you ask when you pray, believe that you receive them, and you will have them" (Mark 11:24, NKJV). I exclaim, "Thank You, Lord, for hearing me! Thank You, Lord, for answering my prayer!" I try to get the whole multitude to rejoice with me, "Clap your hands and shout to God! Thank God that His power is working through you! Shout to God and raise your hands and say, 'Thank You, Lord, for healing me!'" By doing that, I am encouraging the people to enter the supernatural realm of faith with me. I am getting the people to confess their faith. This releases the miracle power of God's Kingdom.

But I'm still not finished. The most critical ingredient still needs to be added. Next, I tell the people, "Now, it's time to act on your faith. Believe in the love of God. Believe in what Jesus accomplished on the cross and act your faith. If you are crippled, get up! Do whatever you could not do. Examine your body. Move in faith. Bend your back, etc." Jesus always told people to act on their faith. He told the cripple to take up his bed and walk. When he did that, he was healed. He told the lepers to go and show themselves to the priests (Luke 17:14). He told the blind man to go wash in the pool of Siloam (John 9:7). He commanded every single individual He healed to do something to activate their faith. Faith with actions produces miracles!

The Essential Step

It's not enough to say, "Get up." It's not sufficient to say, "Touch where you had pain." It's not enough to just say, "Raise your arms!" or "Bend your legs!" You have to demonstrate what you mean. Show the multitude how to act on their faith. If you don't do that, people won't have an example to follow and they'll just stand there and look at you.

I have come to the realization that it doesn't matter whether I am in New York, or New Delhi, if I don't physically demonstrate to the people how to act on their faith, they will rarely move at all. I literally go through the whole gamut of bending, twisting, pantomiming hearing with a deaf ear or seeing with a blind eye, raising crutches up and striding back and forth, pounding on tumors that have disappeared, jumping into the air, and even running in place. When I do this, they follow my example and act on their faith.

When I say, "How many of you are healed? Raise up your hands," sometimes I will see a lot of hands; sometimes I won't see any. But I don't give up. I keep believing the promises of God. I command them to come up in faith, and they come up.

If those of you who are called to this kind of ministry will follow these guidelines, you will begin to experience miracles in your evangelistic ministry as never before. This will work for you! But remember, you have to practice these principles. Maybe at first you won't be very good at this, but don't give up. Keep practicing.

It is paramount that you learn to be skillful in helping people enter the realm of childlike faith. If they believe, they will receive. If they don't believe, they won't receive. Help people believe. This is a powerful message. This is the fountainhead of your power: Faith in God is believing that He loves you!

I have opened up my heart and shared my treasures. I hope you accept them in the spirit in which they have been offered. I would like to pray for everyone who has read this chapter.

❧

Heavenly Father, I pray that these seeds will sink deeply into the hearts of every person who reads this book, that they would put these secrets into action. Thank You that we are anointed. Thank You that we have power. We are part of the beloved; we are Your ambassadors. The devil is under our feet. We believe in You, Lord.

Hallelujah! Thank you Jesus! Amen!

Chapter 5

I Believe in Miracles
Because I Am a Miracle

When I was first saved in such a dramatic and unusual way, 'a lot of people observed me and said, "Oh, there is Osborn's grandson. It's obvious that he was going to be a preacher all along because it's his birthright. It's in his blood." What they don't realize however, is that the first miracle of my ministry was my own miracle.

The devil really tried to destroy me and I was cooperating with him. It was only when I started cooperating with God that I could walk in my birthright. Likewise, God can't do big things with you unless you cooperate with His plan. My cooperation with God made the miracle of my salvation possible.

The Bible says, "As He is, so are we in this world" (1 John 4:17, NKJV). Jesus said, "As the Father has sent Me, I also send you" (John 20:21, NKJV). As you and I cooperate with Him, we become ambassadors for Christ and our ministry reveals the miracles He has done for us. Has God saved you? If so, He wants to save others through you. Has He healed you? If so, He wants to heal others through you. Has He helped you? If so, let Him help others through you. Let Him feed the hungry and visit the sick and the prisoners through you. Let Him love through you, deliver through you, and bless through you!

This is what ministry is. God reveals Himself to us so He might reveal Himself through us to others. Everything God has given us, He wants to share through us. He wants to use us as a channel of His healing power.

The great mystery of the Gospel is "Christ in you, the hope of glory" (Colossians 1:27, NKJV). That is why I say that we are the answer to the world's problems. We are the solution. We are the medicine for the world's ills. We have the cure for crime. We have the cure for AIDS. We have the cure for cancer. We have the answer for mental illness. We have the power of deliverance. We have the solution for all of mankind's problems because what God does to us, He wants to do through us. Jesus said, "Freely you have received, freely give" (Matthew 10:8, NKJV).

Shine Your Light in the Darkness

A lot of people think that somehow they're less effective when they go to a place where there is a lot of spiritual darkness or witchcraft. They don't understand this simple truth that I call the "parallel of the light." If you light a candle and walk outside during the daytime or hold it up in a well-lit church with the sun shining through the windows, it is not going to make much difference. But if you're in a remote village someplace at midnight and there is no moon or any electric lights, your candle will shine the brightest.

When you go out into the darkest spiritual places, God's light shines the brightest. That is where you can make the most difference. That is where your light really shines. The Bible says that where sin abounds, grace does much more abound (Romans 5:20). That means that our light shines the brightest where the darkness is the greatest. When we carry our light to the places where there are Muslims or idol worshippers or where there is a lot of sin, demons or witchcraft, our light shines even brighter. We are not diminished by the darkness. We are more powerful because of the contrast of light and dark, therefore, we can minister with more effectiveness.

Most Christians spend all of their lives shining their candles out in the full sunlight or in places where there is already plenty of light. Why is this? I believe it is because they are afraid of the darkness; they don't have full confidence in the Light. The Bible says the light shines in the darkness and the darkness could not quench or extinguish it (John 1:5). Believe in the Light of Christ in you. Believe in its power. The darkness is nothing compared to the Light. Evil is nothing compared to good. This is literally true.

I am going to say something philosophical that is going to make you think a little bit. Thinking is good! It's good to use your brain. God gave you your brain. Think about this: What is darkness, anyway? Darkness does not exist as an actual thing. Darkness is simply the absence of light. So where there is no light, there is darkness. Darkness is not real in the same sense that light is real. Light is existent. You can do something with it. You can believe in it. In fact, the Bible says God is light (1 John 1:5, NKJV).

We don't have to fear the darkness, even though Satan is the author of spiritual darkness. Satan wants to keep people from the Light of Christ. But what happens to darkness when light shines? It disappears! Darkness cannot coexist with light. Darkness has no actual existence, so we don't have to dread it. All we need to do is to keep shining the light. When people are in darkness, they can't see. They don't know what to do and their actions are without any real coordination. When we shine the light, we expel the darkness. There is an old saying that is true and powerful: "Don't curse the darkness; shine the light!" Light is the only answer to darkness. The only way to fight a lie is with truth. The only way to overcome wickedness is with love.

How do you shine the light? Preach Jesus! Announce the Gospel. The Gospel is the message of light that illuminates the darkness. Darkness disappears when the light of the Good News shines. Darkness can't exist when there is light in a room. I want to shine the light of Jesus into the darkest places in the world, don't you? I want to go forth boldly with courage, fearlessly shining the light of God's love wherever the darkness prevails.

Evil does not exist as a real thing, just as darkness does not exist as a real thing. What? How can that be true? It is true because all evil is really good that has been twisted or perverted. Evil does not have any actual existence because the devil can't create anything. Only God can create. The devil can't create. He is essentially non-creative.

We read in the book of Genesis that God created everything and He said that it was good. Then Satan came along and messed up what God had created. We can see this in satanic art, which is derivative, plagiaristic, and unoriginal. When the devil rebelled against God, he severed himself from God's being, which is essentially creative. Since we are created in the image of God, we share that same desire for creation. The devil does not possess the creative impulse and has rebelled against the Author of everything that is beautiful. All he can do is corrupt that which was essentially created to be good. He takes something perfect and perverts it. There is nothing evil that God didn't intend as good.

How do you overcome evil? The Bible says, "Overcome evil with good" (Romans 12:21, NKJV). We don't have to be terrified of the demonic, occult or any manifestation of spiritual darkness because we have the real thing. We don't have to panic in the presence of evil because we have the One who is the true Light. Each one of us has been indwelt by the light-giving Spirit of the Most High God.

Our Purpose Is One

The sole purpose of our lives is to bring people to Jesus. The Body of Christ is composed of many individuals. We have many different roles to play, but we need to be single-minded in our purpose. The Bible lists the gifts of the Holy Spirit, explaining there are diversities of operation but there is one Lord:

> *"Now concerning spiritual gifts, brethren, I do not want you to be ignorant: You know that you were Gentiles, carried away to these dumb idols, however you were led. Therefore I make known to you that no one speaking by the Spirit of God calls Jesus accursed, and no one can say that Jesus is Lord except by the Holy Spirit. There are diversities of gifts, but the same Spirit. There are differences of ministries, but the same Lord. And there are diversities of activities, but it is the same God who works all in all. But the manifestation of the Spirit is given to each one for the profit of all: for to one is given the word of wisdom through the Spirit, to another the word of knowledge through the same Spirit, to another faith by the same Spirit, to another gifts of healings by the same Spirit, to another the working of miracles, to another prophecy, to another discerning of spirits, to another different kinds of tongues, to another the interpretation of tongues. But one and the same Spirit works all these things, distributing to each one individually as He wills. For as the body is one and has many members, but all the members of that one body, being many, are one body, so also is Christ (1 Corinthians 12:1–13, NKJV).*

There are many different gifts, styles and ministries, but we have to remember that the purpose is always singular. The sole purpose is to make people beautiful like Jesus. If you are a minister of music, you are first a soul-winner—a rescuer of souls. If you are a pastor, you are a rescuer of souls. If you are a teacher, you are a rescuer of souls.

A soccer team has a goalie, defensive players, and forwards. There are many different positions in soccer, but they all work together to accomplish the same purpose: Winning the game. Soccer players do not have ten goals; they have only one—scoring the most goals. It is the same with the body of Christ. We have one goal: To win people to Jesus and help them reflect His light. We reach the lost in order to liberate them for eternity. We desire to make disciples. That is our goal!

I am a singer and a guitar player. I'm also a preacher and have a healing ministry. One person can have more than one skill or talent. Look at the apostle Paul, who wrote that passage about the gifts of the Spirit. He didn't give us that list of gifts so he could exclude people or narrow them down to only one gift. Think about it, Paul himself had the gift of prophecy, discerning of spirits, word of wisdom, word of knowledge, the gift of faith, the gift of healing, and probably more. He had all of those gifts in one person.

Definitely, some people have more gifts than others. And yet because we are all different parts of the body, we have only one purpose: To evangelize the world. We must always remember our goal. In our physical bodies, if one of our arms suddenly wanted to go this way and the other arm wanted to go that way, what could we accomplish? If one of our legs wanted to go its own way opposite from the other leg, we wouldn't get anywhere, would we?

If everyone on a football team just ran around, nobody would ever win a game. It is important for the universal body of Christ to maintain its focus, always operating for God's grand purpose and not being distracted with inconsequential matters. Remember, everything God does to you, He wants to do through you. Keep your eyes on the Lord. He saved you and He will help you shine your light where the darkness seems to be the most impenetrable.

The Pig Woman

The Light of Jesus in believers will shatter the darkness. That's what it did with the woman everybody knew as the Pig Woman. When the Pig Woman walked into the service, every head turned. In the remote West African city where we were conducting a crusade, everyone recognized her face. At one time or another, they had all seen her roaming the streets. She was a mad woman—crazy! She had been that way for years. In fact, she was so disturbed that she actually lived and ate among the swine. That's why the townsfolk called her the Pig Woman.

That night as she entered the packed sanctuary, it was obvious to everyone that she did not belong. She was dressed in rags that barely covered her frail body. Her hair was dirty and matted. The stench was almost unbearable. Her eyes were glazed and her movements were like those of a hunted animal, not a human.

At the climax of my message, the Pig Woman was escorted to the podium. Seeing her sad condition, I stretched out my hand toward her with compassion and declared in a confident voice,

"In the name of Jesus, I command you to come out of her." That instant, her body flew backward as though someone hit her square in the forehead with a two-by-four. Her legs shot out in front of her and she crashed to the floor.

Witnesses gasped in shock. For a moment, no one could tell if she was dead or alive. Everybody ran forward to see what had just happened. When the commotion subsided, I bent down and helped her back to her feet. As she rose, her eyes opened. They were no longer animal-like; instead, they were full of tears. She softly whispered, "They're gone . . . *gone!*"

Emerging from the crowd, my wife, Elisabeth, opened her arms to embrace this woman. However, now aware of her unkempt state, the Pig Woman froze and stiffened against this kind gesture. She thought her smell would offend my wife, but Elisabeth did not let go of her. Instead, she held her even closer and said, "Now we're sisters." As the woman realized that she was now part of the family of God, she held Elisabeth closer and cried.

Chapter 6

Know Your Enemy

When a couple is newly married, they are friends and respect each other. They believe in each other and allow each other to express the gifts of God in their lives. That is a beautiful thing. Sometimes however, it doesn't matter how "Christian" someone is, there will be conflict between a man and a woman. However, the way they handle the conflict will determine whether or not they have success discovering who their real enemy is.

Husbands, the real enemy will never be your wife. Wives, the real enemy will never be your husband. The real enemy is Satan. So instead of fighting against each other, you both need to turn around and fight, shoulder to shoulder, against your real enemy—the devil. Together in faith, you need to submit to God and attack the devil.

It's the same way in ministry; we have to recognize who our true enemy is. Our true enemy is not another person, even if that other person is acting against us with evil motives. Remember, the devil uses people. (Probably, at times, he has even used you!) But the enemy is not you or me; the enemy is the devil.

We need to use spiritual weapons to fight Satan and his evil forces. The Bible says that the weapons of our warfare are not natural, physical weapons. They are supernatural, spiritual weapons (2 Corinthians 10:4). Our weapons are spiritual. That means our victory will be a spiritual one, too!

The Bible tells us that "the reason the Son of God appeared was to destroy the devil's work" (1 John 3:8, NIV), and "God anointed Jesus of Nazareth with the Holy Spirit and with power, who went about doing good and healing all who were oppressed by the devil, for God was with Him" (Acts 10:38, NKJV). Jesus recognized that His enemy (and ours) is Satan. When He went to the cross, His death bought our complete victory over Satan's evil manipulation.

The devil is afraid of you because when he looks in your eyes, which are the windows of your soul (Matthew 6:22–23), he sees Jesus. The redemptive name of the Lord is *Jehovah Nissi,* which means "the Lord our banner" or "the Lord our victory." The Lord wants us to have victory and success in our lives. Every time I preach the Gospel, I carry the banner of victory into battle. I am triumphant with Jehovah Nissi. Demons tremble, sickness is driven out, people are healed, and I have victory, because Jesus has already purchased victory by His death and resurrection.

Many Christians do not understand redemption. Redemption is the reality that Jesus purchased our complete victory over the kingdom of darkness: sin, sickness, bondage, depression, evil, and fear. Jesus purchased *us*. Now we can live in the reality of redemption because we have been redeemed from the enemy. Believers who do not comprehend this redemptive truth are still living in the old covenant. They live in terror of God because they do not realize they have been made righteous by the blood of Jesus. When they pray, you can tell by their long, miserable prayers that they don't really get it. They say, "Oh Lord, I am a sinner....I am weak....I cannot do anything.... Save me from the devil.... The devil is after me...." God hates those kinds of prayers because He already paid the price for our redemption.

Pharisees prayed long prayers, but Jesus rebuked them saying, "Woe to you, scribes and Pharisees, hypocrites! For you devour widows' houses, and for a pretense make long prayers. Therefore you will receive greater condemnation" (Matthew 23:14, NKJV). Every prayer we pray should be a redemptive prayer. Simply speaking, every prayer should reflect the truth that Jesus paid for each one of us to be ransomed out of Satan's power. We walk in love, faith, and victory because His Spirit lives inside our hearts. We have been redeemed! Jesus has purchased our total redemption for all time.

Jesus defeated the devil once and for all, so now we can walk in victory. We can carry the banner of victory wherever we go because, "He has put all things under His feet" (1 Corinthians 15:27, NKJV). By revelation, I know that Jesus lives in me and all the works of darkness are under my feet. Jesus purchased our victory on the cross, not for Himself but for us! Now all things of the devil are under our dominion.

No Longer Under the Law

People who don't understand their redemption are Old Testament people. Old Testament people live in bondage under the law. They are afraid that if they do something wrong, God will kill them. They think if they think a wrong thought, speak a wrong word, or do something wrong, they will go to hell when they die. They are always worried about outward things. They are worried about clothes, hairstyles, and genres of music, literature and art. They are apprehensive of how people look at them. They are worried about what they eat. They are always concerned with outward ceremony. That is Old Testament.

Because of Jesus, we have left that behind us. "And you, . . . He has made alive together with Him, having forgiven you all trespasses, having wiped out the handwriting of requirements that was against us, which was contrary to us. And He has taken it out of the way, having nailed it to the cross. Having disarmed principalities and powers, He made a public spectacle of them, triumphing over them in it" (Colossians 2:13–15, NKJV).

When Jesus died on the cross, all of that bondage of ritual and ceremony, law, animal sacrifices, and all of those terrible things were nailed to the cross. When Jesus hung on the cross, He said, "IT IS FINISHED!" Religion was finished. The requirements of the law had been fulfilled in His ultimate blood sacrifice.

Jesus was not religious. He did not come to bring more religion. He came to fulfill the Old Testament and take religion out of the way. He came to fulfill the law and declare, "It is finished!" This means that the old covenant is dead. If you are living in the old covenant, you are living in death. When you come over to the new covenant, you come into liberty. When you encourage somebody else to come over to the new covenant, you invite them into the liberty of redemption.

Jesus has delivered us from the bondage of the law and has enabled us to walk in the liberty of grace. In every sense of the word, He has defeated the true enemy. He spoiled, He destroyed, He conquered all the demonic armies that were arrayed against Him and us, and He made a public demonstration of their defeat. He completely triumphed over them. His victory is our victory! His life is our life! His righteousness is our righteousness! His power is our power! His love is our love! His health is our health!

We are destined to win this perpetual war that is raging—the struggle against good and evil, excellence and mediocrity, love and fear, health and disease, and success and failure. We have to remember that the devil, our adversary, is relentless. He never quits.

But, the devil no longer has any real power over us. He is a liar. His power is the power of lies. He comes to deceive, cheat, steal, obstruct, condemn, and accuse. He sows doubt in God's promises. He tells us the promises of God are not applicable in our case. These lies are the only power he has over us. He is our enemy. If we know who we are in Jesus then Satan is under our feet.

The devil uses ignorance as one of his chief weapons. We are vulnerable through our ignorance. The devil seeks to steal the seed of truth from our hearts, making us vulnerable and prone to failure. That's why we must resist mediocrity and slavery. Defeat is never God's plan for His people.

Satan wants us to blame the things of God on the devil and the things of the devil on God. This happened to Jesus. He healed people and they turned around and said that He healed people by the power of Satan. "Then they brought him a demon-possessed man who was blind and mute, and Jesus healed him, so that he could both talk and see. All the people were astonished and said, 'Could this be the Son of David?' But when the Pharisees heard this, they said, 'It is only by Beelzebul, the prince of demons, that this fellow drives out demons.' Jesus knew their thoughts and said to them, 'Every kingdom divided against itself will be ruined, and every city or household divided against itself will not stand. If Satan drives out Satan, he is divided against himself. How then can his kingdom stand? And if I drive out demons by Beelzebul, by whom do your people drive them out?'" (Matthew 12:22-27, NIV).

Jesus, the Captain of Our Salvation

We have to resist the devil and submit ourselves to God (James 4:7). However, some people do the opposite; they resist God and submit to the devil. Jesus Christ is the Captain of our salvation (Hebrews 2:1–10). Salvation comes from the Greek word *sozo*, which means to be saved, to be healed, to be rescued, to be made safe, to have deliverance, to have victory. Salvation includes victory, liberty, righteousness, peace, and protection. If you understand what salvation includes, the Bible comes alive in new ways. Consider the following passages. I have emphasized the word "salvation" and "saved" in each one:

> ". . . *having been perfected, He [Jesus] became the author of eternal **salvation** to all who obey Him" (Hebrews 5:9, NKJV; brackets and emphasis mine).*

> *"How shall we escape if we ignore so great a **salvation**? This **salvation**, which was first announced by the Lord, was confirmed to us by those who heard him. God also testified to it by signs, wonders and various miracles, and by gifts of the Holy Spirit distributed according to his will" (Hebrews 2:3–4, NIV; emphasis mine).*

> *"Praise be to the God and Father of our Lord Jesus Christ! In his great mercy he has given us new birth into a living hope through the resurrection of Jesus Christ from the dead, and into an inheritance that can never perish, spoil or fade. This inheritance is kept in heaven for you, who through faith are shielded by God's power until the coming of the **salvation** that is ready to be revealed in the last time" (1 Peter 1:3–5, NIV; emphasis mine).*

> *"Since we belong to the day, let us be sober, putting on faith and love as a breastplate, and the hope of **salvation** as a helmet. For God did not appoint us to suffer wrath but to receive **salvation***

through our Lord Jesus Christ. He died for us so that, whether we are awake or asleep, we may live together with him" (1 Thessalonians 5:8–10, NIV; emphasis mine).

*"Take the helmet of **salvation** and the sword of the Spirit, which is the word of God" (Ephesians 6:17, NIV; emphasis mine).*

*"Know this, you and all the people of Israel: It is by the name of Jesus Christ of Nazareth, whom you crucified but whom God raised from the dead, that this man stands before you healed. Jesus is 'the stone you builders rejected, which has become the cornerstone.' **Salvation** is found in no one else, for there is no other name under heaven given to mankind by which we must be **saved**" (Acts 4:10–12, NIV; emphasis mine).*

*"For it is with your heart that you believe and are justified, and it is with your mouth that you profess your faith and are **saved**" (Romans 10:10, NIV; emphasis mine).*

Jesus, our Savior, the Captain of our salvation, leads us to victory. Everywhere we go, the Captain of our salvation goes with us. When the devil looks at us, he does not see a loser. He sees Jesus—the One who defeated and crushed him. When I stand on a platform in the name of Jesus, I don't see a lot of demons that can hurt me; I see a lot of needy people who have been bound by demons. I have the authority to set them free by the power of the Gospel. I have a feeling the demons tremble and are afraid because they know the moment I use the name of Jesus, they are going to be blasted away by the power of the Holy Ghost.

All of our victory is in Jesus. We have abundant living through Jesus. Jesus said, "The thief does not come except to steal, and to kill, and to destroy. I have come that they may have life, and that they may have it more abundantly" (John 10:10, NKJV). The apostle Paul wrote, "We are more than conquerors through him who loved us" (Romans 8:37, NIV).

It would be good enough to have a God who was just a conqueror, but not only has Jesus Christ conquered death and ultimate punishment, He always causes us to triumph over darkness. Jesus is our Captain; our salvation is complete. Christ's triumph is our triumph. He arose in total victory over our adversary, Satan. When Christ was raised from the dead, we were raised along with Him by the operation of the love of God. And "If God is for us, who can be against us?" (Romans 8:31, NKJV).

In Revelation 1:17-18 (NKJV), Jesus said, "Do not be afraid; I am the First and the Last. I am He who lives, and was dead, and behold, I am alive forevermore, Amen. And I have the keys of Hades and of Death." This same Jesus is in me and you. *His* authority is *our* authority. Jesus' authority over sickness and sin is demonstrated every time we preach the Gospel.

Takoradi Crusade

Here is a report of a modern miracle that happened at one of our crusades in Africa, in Takoradi, Ghana. Night after night, a field of eager Africans gathered to witness the spectacular evidence of Jesus' resurrection and to hear the wonderful Good

News of the Kingdom of God. Thousands received Jesus nightly as we shouted joyfully, "The Kingdom of God has come upon you!" I preached, "They that are whole have no need of the physician, but they that are sick: I came not to call the righteous, but sinners to repentance" (Mark 2:17, KJV). To the amazement of the people, blind eyes received sight, deaf ears popped open, the crippled rose and walked, and even the insane were delivered and made well.

A man named Yow Sakyi had been possessed by demons for ten years. When the devils came into him a decade before, something terrible began to happen. The demons would unexpectedly oppress him and make him insane. He testified that the demons within him would urge him to kill people, even his own brother. When he felt most overcome by the madness, he would shake violently and walk for miles not knowing where he was going. Then when he came to himself, he would find himself in some strange town.

Voices tormented him, saying, "Today you're going to die!" Other times, the demons would oppress his body and make him feel unbearably cold and he would try to gather blankets from everywhere to cover himself, but all in vain. His life was a never-ending nightmare. He was so troubled that he had never even learned to read or write, even though he was a very intelligent man.

On the fifth night of the crusade as he heard the Word of God, he felt a physical manifestation of something like cold water drenching his whole body, pouring from his head straight down to his feet. The tormenting spirits were being driven out of him as I commanded them to go in Jesus' name. He came trembling to the platform and shouted, "Jesus has set me free!" Through a translator, he gave his wonderful testimony of how he had received Jesus and how the evil spirits fled from him.

The people were full of excitement as Yow spoke about this great miracle. After he gave his testimony, I reached up (because he's a very tall young man) and laid my hand on his head and prayed for him to be filled with the Holy Spirit. He crashed down on the platform with tremendous force. (Later he told us that he felt as if someone had gently laid him down in a cool and peaceful place.) After he lay as if he were dead for quite some time, he put his hands up in the air and started praising God in other tongues for the very first time. The people were amazed. Yow's life had been translated from the kingdom of darkness into the Kingdom of God's dear Son!

The next day as Yow told us his testimony, he declared, "I am going to preach the Gospel with miracles just like Evangelist O'Dell." And I believe he will. God is now his master and He will dethrone Satan wherever Yow goes and preaches the Good News.

Who was Yow's real enemy? Mental illness? The evil suggestions he tried to resist? No! Satan was his real enemy. Today, Satan is still his enemy, just like he is your and my enemy. But now, like us, because of Jesus Christ, Yow can rejoice in complete freedom from the evil power of the enemy's voice.

Chapter 7

Confessions of Power

At one of our Argentina miracle meetings, I was preaching from the platform when a woman came in to destroy me. She had been a witch for many years, heavily involved in practicing witchcraft and black magic. As she entered the room, her intention was to put a curse on me. But immediately when she saw me, she knew she was not going to be able to harm me. The demons inside of her knew the power of Jesus Christ was present in me, and they became fearful and agitated in His presence. The chief demon actually spoke through her saying, "I want to destroy you, but I can't." Then I asked her if she wanted to be free. Without hesitation she replied, "Yes!"

In the name of Jesus, I commanded the evil spirits to leave her, and without any argument, the devils left. Then I prayed for her to be filled with the Holy Ghost. The next day she got rid of everything connected to her witchcraft practices. She killed three snakes with her bare hands and put all of her witchcraft books into a fire and burned them up. As she was doing this, an invisible evil power suddenly came and lifted her off the ground and threw her against the wall. She said she did not even have to think but with the supernatural guidance of the Holy Spirit, she spoke the words, "In Jesus' name I resist you!" Immediately the evil force left, leaving her victorious in Christ.

This true story illustrates the power of confession. When we confess the name of Jesus out loud, His authority prevails over all evil. The Holy Spirit within us will help us make a habit of confessing the truth about Jesus.

A Powerful Confession

Here is a confession for you to read out loud. This powerful confession is about righteousness. Why start by confessing righteousness? We should confess righteousness because Jesus' righteousness and the righteousness He has transferred to us is such a significant revelation. If you confess your righteousness in Jesus, you can enter into the blessings He came to bring you. You can receive supernatural miracles and every kind of victory. If you feel condemned, accused, vile or no good, you do not identify with redemption. You are still living in the Old Testament.

It's imperative to understand Christ's redemptive work in order to understand the righteousness we have received from God. The righteousness that was transferred to us by Jesus' death on the cross accomplishes our redemption. Legally, all of the debt of unrighteousness was laid to Christ's account and all of the righteousness in His account was laid to our account. Jesus' righteousness guarantees our salvation. When you lay hold of this by a confession of faith, you can enter the door to the Kingdom of God. Then all the other blessings of redemption can come to you. If you fail to understand the importance of Jesus' righteousness, you cannot receive anything else.

When you can say, "I am righteous because He is righteous" and believe it, then you can become a person living in the new covenant. This will radically alter your lifestyle. You will leave dead works behind and move forward into a living, loving, victorious relationship with your Father. Say this confession out loud:

God, You have revealed Yourself by Your redemptive name, Jehovah Tsidkenu, which means, the Lord my Righteousness. Lord Jesus, You have ransomed me with Your precious blood, now the way is open for me to receive the perfect gift of righteousness. I have dignity that can never be compromised. You gave Your life for me and brought me back to friendship with God. There is now no judgment, no curse, no condemnation for me because I am restored to oneness with God. Because I am restored to oneness with God, I have no sense of guilt.

If you understand what you have just read aloud, all the other miracles of redemption will be easy. This is the hardest one—understanding that you are righteous and have oneness with God. Everything else is simple by comparison. You will no longer have a sense of unworthiness. You will no longer feel inadequate to pray or unworthy of receiving answers.

Sin consciousness undermines our faith and dignity. People who are living in sin consciousness tend to have a problem with temptation. In essence, they are confessing sin instead of righteousness. Because they say and believe they are sinners, they live in sin consciousness and have no revelation of righteousness. They do not understand the purpose of the blood of Jesus. Sin consciousness produces feelings of inadequacy and inferiority that lead to depression, which in turn can lead to fear and dread.

The truth is that through Christ's sacrifice, we no longer need to rely on our old religious efforts to be judged righteous or to achieve favor with God. As long as we remain mired in sin consciousness, we will feel like we need to pray harder, fast more often, and work harder to keep seeking God's favor. But none of this makes us more righteous.

Our righteousness comes from the blood of Jesus. We can now pray, fast, work and seek God because of the miracle of our redemption from sin consciousness. Something happened inside of us that made us righteous, but we did not earn it. Jesus did. Jesus, who never sinned, achieved righteousness for us. He made Himself a substitute for us on the Father's scales of judgment. If we could have saved ourselves, Jesus wouldn't have needed to die for us.

Confessing Freedom

Here is another confession that you can say aloud by faith:

I have been created to walk with God, to have personal communion with my Heavenly Father. Jesus' righteousness has been imputed to me. It has been infused into me. Now my nature has become Christ's nature. I have regained my sense of righteousness. The power of sin-consciousness has been destroyed. Along with it, all of my torment has been destroyed. Now I can enter again into God's presence. I am no longer haunted by the guilt that produced and that was produced by a lifestyle of spiritual darkness. I am now free of the lifestyle of failure. I am free to walk with God. All my sins were charged to Christ's account. All of His righteousness has been legally transferred to my account. I am a royal member of the family of God. I am a child of the High King. My personal dignity has been restored.

I salute you for making this important confession. When you receive and accept it, you come in through the door of righteousness. That's when the entire compendium of the Lord's blessings can flow into you. You will be able to confess His greatness with enthusiasm. You will be able to quote His truths from His Word, the Bible, and as a result you will find yourself calling Him by His redemptive names.

If you start feeling condemned again, you will revisit the revelation of *Jehovah Tsidkenu,* the Lord our Righteousness. When you feel defeated and recognize you need a victory, you will remember that another one of His names is the Lord our Banner of Victory, *Jehovah Nissi.* When you or someone else needs His healing touch, confess Him as *Jehovah Rapha,* the Lord that Heals.

He meets your every need. You have to agree that everything He does constitutes a miracle. He is *Jehovah Rah,* the Lord our

Shepherd. Every time you are lonely and need a friend, He is *Jehovah Shama,* which means the Lord is Present. He is here. He will never leave you. He will never forsake you. He will be a friend that sticks closer than a brother (Hebrews 13:5; Proverbs 18:24).

If you or someone else needs a material miracle, you can take your request to *Jehovah Jireh,* the Lord our Provider. He is much more than a God of material miracles. When you are afraid and need a miracle of peace, He is *Jehovah Shalom,* the Lord our Peace. Every kind of miracle we need comes from the redemption of God that Jesus accomplished completely on the cross—every miracle, not just healing.

His love is unlimited. His redemption is unlimited. His blessings and favor are unlimited. His grace is unlimited. You can experience the glory of God today as you allow the seeds He has sown in your heart to sprout up and bear fruit.

Chapter 8

People Are Eternal

The people you meet every day are eternal. The question is, where will each one of them spend eternity? Once you have that question settled in your own life and you are filled with the Spirit of God, it's time to start paving the way to glory for others. The apostle Paul put it this way: "For what is our hope, our joy, or the crown in which we will glory in the presence of our Lord Jesus when he comes? Is it not you?" (1 Thessalonians 2:19, NIV). When I think of all the marvels we have seen and the beautiful miracles we have witnessed, the greatest thing of all is the millions of precious people we have won into the Kingdom of God.

There are hundreds of miracles at our crusades. We are moved by the desperate need of the hurting, suffering, unreached people, and infused with the compassion of God. As the Spirit of God moves into the place, we see a beautiful thing—people who came in with no hope, whose hope is like a candle long extinguished, receive that first flickering flame of hope resurrected. People who have been enslaved in Satan's kingdom for generations because their parents, grandparents, and great-grandparents all lived and died without ever hearing the Good News, begin to discover for the first time that they are free. Imagine what that's like. They don't have to be tormented anymore in fear because of witchcraft. They don't have to serve dead gods anymore. Most of all, they don't have to be lost anymore. They don't have to live in a meaningless universe where there is no God. They don't have to live day to day in a place where there is no truth or foundation—nothing to lean on, no life, and no love.

Isaac Lamptey

At the Frontier Evangelism crusade in Takoradi, Ghana, God demonstrated His love for each person. I want to tell you about several individuals so you can rejoice and know that what God is willing to do for one, He is willing to do for everyone.

A modern-day miracle was performed by the unchanging Christ Jesus for an old man named Isaac Lamptey. Isaac was seventy-five years old. He had suffered a stroke a few years previously that had paralyzed him totally on one side. Both his eyes and ears were also affected. He had lost almost all of his sight and all of his hearing because of the stroke.

Somehow he found out about the crusade, in spite of not being able to hear the announcements on the radio or read the posters or newspaper. The first day he arrived many hours too early, expecting what had been advertised so boldly—a miracle of God.

My wife, Elisabeth, happened to be at the grounds earlier than anyone on that first night and saw Isaac coming. He had a walking stick and was wearing dark glasses. Another man assisted him as he hobbled to the crusade inch by inch, resting every few feet. The man with him carried a little stool that Isaac would collapse on every few steps, exhausted by the strain of his efforts.

It seemed to take ages for him to finally reach the crusade grounds. Isaac brought his stool close to the platform, sat down slowly, and waited for hours until it was time for the meeting to start. In the meantime, thousands of people gathered. The atmosphere was charged with anticipation to see and hear the great event that had been announced so boldly. I got up to preach and was anointed with the Holy Ghost. Even though he probably couldn't hear me, Isaac's hope was kindled into faith by the time I gave the invitation to become a child of God.

When Isaac later told his story, he said, "When Evangelist O'Dell shouted that this was the time to receive Christ in my life, I did. And at that moment, something moved through my body and I received total healing! I felt strong again and my eyes and ears were also opened!"

Isaac rushed to the platform to give his testimony as the first witness of many. He gave his testimony, full of love and power. The people listened with astonishment. After he finished, he demonstrated his healing in every way possible. The crowd burst forth with praise to God. What happened to Isaac gave them undeniable proof that Jesus Christ is risen from the dead and is alive and unchanged today.

Isaac told his fellow Ghanaians how he had gone to witch doctors for years, but all in vain. Nothing had ever changed, except that he grew worse. "Now," he said, "I am proof to you that Jesus Christ is alive. Receive Him, and never visit our traditional healers again. Jesus is the answer!" What a testimony from someone newly saved! The people gladly accepted his advice and praised God once again.

Isaac came almost every night after that and was seated on the platform. When it was time for prayer for the sick he would get up and march all over the platform, kicking his legs, stretching his arms, dancing and moving to remind the people what Jesus had done for him. He wanted to show them that if God had done it for one old man, He would do it for anyone.

Miracles like that one keep me on the road proclaiming the Good News. Our message is rooted in faith. Our faith is rooted in love. Our love is rooted in the revelation of what Jesus did for us on the cross and what He continues to do as our intercessor, High Priest, Advocate, and Captain of our salvation. Every song we sing, every word we say, and every message we preach is a triumphant declaration of liberty for the captives.

The Eyes of the Blind Shall Be Opened

The prophet Isaiah wrote:

"The wilderness and the wasteland shall be glad for them,
And the desert shall rejoice and blossom as the rose;
It shall blossom abundantly and rejoice,

Even with joy and singing. . . .
. . . Strengthen the weak hands,
And make firm the feeble knees.
Say to those who are fearful-hearted,
'Be strong, do not fear!
Behold, your God will come with vengeance,
With the recompense of God;
He will come and save you.'
Then the eyes of the blind shall be opened,
And the ears of the deaf shall be unstopped.
Then the lame shall leap like a deer,
And the tongue of the dumb sing."
(Isaiah 35:1–2, 3–6, NKJV)

My life was a wilderness until Jesus came. It was like the parched, forbidding wilderness in the Middle East where this was written by Isaiah. In the Middle East, "wilderness" refers to deserts where nothing wholesome grows, only thorns and poisonous plants. That's what my life was like before Jesus came in to it. Yet, even in this wilderness, living waters sprang forth, creating streams. Spiritually, that is what happens to us when the Living Water of God comes. Isaiah went on to say,

"For waters shall burst forth in the wilderness,
And streams in the desert.
The parched ground shall become a pool,
And the thirsty land springs of water;

In the habitation of jackals, where each lay,
There shall be grass with reeds and rushes.
A highway shall be there, and a road,
And it shall be called the Highway of Holiness.
The unclean shall not pass over it,
But it shall be for others.
Whoever walks the road, although a fool,
Shall not go astray.
No lion shall be there,
Nor shall any ravenous beast go up on it;
It shall not be found there.
But the redeemed shall walk there,
And the ransomed of the LORD shall return,
And come to Zion with singing,
With everlasting joy on their heads.
They shall obtain joy and gladness,
And sorrow and sighing shall flee away."
(Isaiah 35:6–10, NKJV)

In the dry land of our souls, in our desert that has never known water, the ground cracks open and geysers start shooting through the ground. Streams fill the land with flowing water. Before long, trees burst with new fruit. Our parched ground becomes a pool of water and our thirsty spirits drink from flowing springs of water. The King James translation of Isaiah 35: 7 reads, "And the parched ground shall become a pool, and the thirsty land springs of water: in the habitation of dragons, where each lay, shall be grass with reeds and rushes." Dragons symbolize evil spirits, and it's true—the works of the enemy are scoured from the healed land as well. Now we can lie down and satisfy our thirst in a beautiful, newborn land of reeds and rushes, a complete contrast from the harsh desert we used to live in.

Much of the world is a spiritual desert, a wilderness. Out there, you can find nothing but dry land. There's no Living Water. It is arid and desiccated. Nothing can grow. We keep preaching the Gospel because we see people languishing in spiritual dehydration. As we preach, pray and proclaim the coming of the Kingdom, we are privileged to see streams of living water explode forth. When we see not only new life, but also blind eyes opening, deaf ears unstopping, mute mouths beginning to speak and shout, and lame legs leaping, everyone knows it is real.

Nearly every month I go overseas to hold a major crusade. Whether we are cooperating with local churches or going into an area that has no churches, we make sure the desert gets watered. The refreshing water of the Gospel replenishes everything to overflowing. Jesus said, "Whosoever drinketh of the water that I shall give him shall never thirst; but the water that I shall give him shall be in him a well of water springing up into everlasting life" (John 4:14, KJV). Jesus was the fulfillment of Isaiah's prophetic words, and those words are still true today across the globe. Truly the eyes of the blind shall be opened and the lame shall run and leap for joy.

Here are two more accounts from the Takoradi Crusade. Abena Nkansah had been blind for over fifteen years. Her grandson had heard of the crusade and the miracles that were happening, so he decided to bring his blind grandmother. That night at our crusade as Abena heard to the Good News, she believed that God loved her and wanted to give her sight back.

While I was praying for healing, she covered her eyes with her hands. She believed. Then God did what only He can do—He opened her blind eyes! Ecstatic, she pushed her way through the crowd and climbed up the stairs onto the platform and testified of her healing. When I found out that she had been blind when she came into the meeting, I said, "Do you see my nose?"

She said, "Yes!"

"Then come and get it!" I exclaimed.

Her eyes focused and she grabbed my nose. No problem! Excitedly, she said, "I can see your ears," and she grabbed them, too. "And also your chin," she added, grabbing it. Before I had time to think, she planted a big kiss on my cheek. If only everyone could have seen the joy on her face! God's miracles demonstrate His love in the best way possible.

On another night, a beautiful girl named Marian came to the crusade. She had broken both of her legs in an accident when she was thirteen years old and was in constant pain ever since. Marian was a very promising runner before her accident. On the second night of the crusade, God mightily healed her legs. They were as good as new; they looked like nothing had ever happened to them. She demonstrated her healing by sprinting back and forth on the platform, overwhelmed with joy and thanksgiving to God.

Satisfying Our Hunger

Jesus promised to satisfy our hunger. Jesus said, "For the bread of God is he which cometh down from heaven, and giveth life unto the world. Then said they unto him, Lord, evermore give us this bread. And Jesus said unto them, I am the bread of life: he that cometh to me shall never hunger; and he that believeth on me shall never thirst" (John 6:33–35, KJV).

Jesus suffered for you, personally. He was wounded for *your* transgressions. You can receive healing personally. He was bruised for *your* iniquities. The chastisement of *your* peace was on Him. He bore *your* sickness and carried *your* disease and *your* pain. And by His stripes *you* are healed (Isaiah 53:5). That's real!

I don't think that I am overemphasizing something that is not really all that important. Did you know that seventy-five percent of Jesus' ministry time was spent healing the sick? Everywhere He went, He healed the sick, cast out devils, and helped the needy. Not one time did anyone who came to Jesus for healing or anything else get turned away. He never said, "Not you." Not once. It wasn't even time for the dispensation for the non-Jews, yet He healed non-Jews also.

He gives us bread from heaven when He gives us His gifts. He doesn't take back the gifts He gives us. When I come back to America from one of my trips overseas, I go through customs. The officials stop me and ask if I have any plants or animals, or if I have spent any time on a farm. They also ask if I have any drugs or weapons. But they never ask, "Do you have any gifts of the Spirit?

No, we don't want any of those here. You will have to leave those with me." (I couldn't leave them anyway, even if I wanted to.)

God wants to use you wherever you go. You are an ambassador for Christ. You can experience compassion for people who have never heard the Gospel. You can experience the satisfying, purifying presence of the Lord all the time, everywhere. God is opening deaf ears, healing blind eyes, and causing cancerous growths to disappear not only in Third World countries, but also in America. People are being healed of arthritis and set free from their torments and drugs. Everything God has done to you, He wants to do through you. That's the way it is for me, and He wants it to be that way for you, too.

Chapter 9

Hindu Hostilities and Muslim Miracles

Unreached people are unreached for a reason. A lot of elements make them hard to reach, such as challenging geography, false religions, governments that are antagonistic to the Gospel, strife and persecution. But the power of God always clears the way and we are winning the battle for souls. We are demonstrating Satan's defeat at Calvary. We are going to unreached territories and standing on Satan's turf, proclaiming the Gospel of Jesus Christ.

One day, Jesus cried out in public that if anyone thirsts let him come to Him and drink the water of life freely. He also said that when they drink, out of their heart, rivers of living water would flow! (John 7:37-39). The living water is the Holy Ghost. The living water will flow through the desert wilderness of our hearts and out into any untamed wilderness we go to. That living water brings salvation to unreached people, but they can't be saved unless they hear the Gospel. They won't believe unless they see the Good News confirmed with demonstrations of the gifts of the Holy Ghost.

The Gospel was never supposed to be just some kind of nice philosophy for wise people to sit around debating. Paul said, "My speech and my preaching was not with enticing words of man's wisdom, but in demonstration of the Spirit and of power: That your faith should not stand in the wisdom of men, but in the power of God" (1 Corinthians 2:4–5, KJV).

Challenges in India

In our campaign in Tiruppur, India, I was charged with criminal fraud for practicing medicine without a license and for inciting an uprising. I had to go to their court, where thirty-five lawyers were fighting against me and accusing me before the judge. These lawyers were all radical Hindus. They were irritated that I had the audacity to come to their city and preach Jesus with miracle evidence. They were furious that thousands of devout Hindus believed in Jesus each night, joyfully receiving Him as their Lord.

Thankfully, there was one women lawyer (she was actually married to one of my accusers) who decided to champion me. She stood up for me and requested my case so she could defend me alone against all the others. She'd had a dream the night before, and in that dream, Jesus told her she must defend a man named Tommy O'Dell. So she did. She argued my case against thirty-five radical lawyers of the fanatical BJP party. The BJP wanted anyone who was not a Hindu to be expelled from India—or dead.

God gave my defender supernatural wisdom. When the Hindu lawyers started claiming that I was practicing medicine without a license, she actually opened the Bible to Luke 7:22 (NIV): "Go back and report to John what you have seen and heard: The blind receive sight, the lame walk, those who have leprosy are cleansed, the deaf hear, the dead are raised, and the good news is proclaimed to the poor." She opened the Bible and put it in front of the Hindu judge. He read the Bible in the presence of his court for the first time. When he came to the part where it says "the dead are raised," all thirty-five of the lawyers began to scream, "That's false! That's a myth!"

The judge shouted back, "Don't you call it fraud; this is the Christians' holy book. In India we are taught to respect other people's religions." As he slammed down his gavel, he exclaimed, "This case is dismissed!"

In Tiruppur, we saw ten crippled children who had been paralyzed from birth. All of them were healed and they walked back and forth across the platform to prove it. One blind man whose body was paralyzed by a stroke felt the power of God flow through him. Instantly, his arms and legs were rejuvenated with new life. Then the fire of God burned up through his body and opened his eyes. He was so happy. He said he could feel Jesus in his heart and he knew he was saved. He said, "It is so kind that you came to tell me about Jesus."

This Gospel we preach is not a fairy tale. It's not just a nice story. It's not just another religion. It's real! When we get serious about the Kingdom of God, as the early church did, we will see the same things that they saw.

The healings we saw in Tiruppur were like those in the Book of Acts in the Bible. For instance, a Muslim family brought their dead son to the meeting. The little boy had died as they were on their way to the crusade. He had previously been sick for about six months. Raging with a high fever, he had languished, getting weaker each day, but his parents didn't have enough money to take him to the doctor. His condition had continued to deteriorate as they carried him, walking many hot, dusty miles to the healing meeting because it was their only hope. When they saw their precious son's breathing stop and his eyes roll back in his head as his skin grew cold, they moaned in anguish. Yet, they kept walking.

They were dismayed when they reached the crusade. As far as they could see, there were thousands of people packed together. I was standing on the rough wooden platform, unaware of the boy's death. I was only aware of all the insects that the halogen lights were attracting. Every time I preach at a crusade, bugs fly around my head and sometimes one ends up in my mouth. When that happens, I just eat it and keep smiling and preaching. Even if the climate is hot and humid and the food I ate for dinner is churning in my stomach, I keep smiling. Even if I'm miserable and homesick, I just keep smiling as I preach because that's my life, and God wants to show His power to unreached people.

In this particular meeting, those enemies of the Gospel who wanted to see me dead were in the crowd, but they didn't dare do anything to me because of the thousands of people at the meeting. The crowds liked me because many of them had been healed. We didn't even take up offerings because the people might think I was like their gurus or holy men and would think they were paying for their miracle. We always offer the Gospel freely, not worrying about how we're going to afford it or who's out there in the crowd.

The family brought their dead baby up toward me on the platform. They pushed their way through the thick crowd. It took them a long time to reach us. They kept screaming desperately, always pressing forward. They got up to my crusade helper, who was an Indian man named John Abraham. He had been in charge of the teams who put up the thousands of posters. John is a big, rugged formidable man—a stoic, impressive man. But when they brought the baby's corpse up to him and he saw the little boy's cold, rigid body, the mighty John Abraham turned to jelly.

It wasn't that he was afraid of a dead baby. It was because John knew there were dangerous enemies in the crowd. He knew that even though Indian people can be the loveliest people on earth, they can also be the most volatile. They will riot quicker than any other people group I know. You don't have to be a genius to realize that having someone die at your healing meeting is very bad!

John immediately started working, getting people to arrange a car to take the baby to the hospital so they could arrange for the baby to be buried. He told them we would pay for everything. While he was getting everything organized, something began to rise up inside of his heart. The Bible says, "When the enemy shall come in like a flood, the Spirit of the LORD shall lift up a standard against him" (Isaiah 59:19, KJV). The Spirit of the Lord lifted up a standard against the devil to demonstrate the invincibility of God's Truth. Something like steel rose up in John, and all of a sudden, he became brave and said, "Go back out there and believe God and God will do a miracle." And God did!

When we prayed for the people, we did it all at once as usual. (If we didn't, we would still be there praying because the crowds are so huge.) The power of God moved mightily over the people and many were powerfully healed. Many blind eyes opened, tumors disappeared, cancers were healed, cripples walked, and demon-possessed people were freed.

A woman from a very high Brahman family, who was demon-possessed and had a tumor in her throat, was totally delivered and healed.

The Muslim parents of the dead baby prayed and to their astonishment, their baby was alive again! He started moving around actively. The fever was gone! He had been raised from the dead and healed. They brought him up in front of all the people and just wept. Their expressions didn't change much because Indians are not very expressive emotionally. They just stood there with tears bathing their faces. They declared in front of all the people, "Now, we believe that Jesus is the Messiah, that He has been raised from the dead. We will serve Him as long as we live."

Muslim Miracles

If you and I had grown up in Somalia, Afghanistan or Kazakhstan, chances are we would be Muslims. We would probably think and speak the same way as they do. We would probably fear and hate Christianity, along with all of Western civilization. I have real compassion for Muslims because when they hear the Gospel of Jesus Christ with the experience of accompanying miracles and supernatural evidence, they will throw down everything they have ever believed and accept Jesus. It is the same way for Buddhists, Hindus, animists or Shinto people. Just as in a court case, those who want the truth will accept the winning evidence. Their hearts open up and they receive God's amazing grace.

One time I was preaching in western Ghana in a place called Buaku. At the time, this region was very dark, less than one percent Christian. A gang of radical Muslims took a blood oath that they wouldn't eat until they killed me. They came to the first meeting armed to the teeth, prepared to kill me. They planned to watch and strike after I finished preaching and praying, when I asked those who had been healed to testify on the platform. They assumed I would pretend that people were healed and present fake miracles to the Muslim audience.

Isn't it amazing that those unsophisticated villagers in Buaku would have the same cynical attitude as unbelieving American atheists? People are the same everywhere; human nature is universal. Cultures, attitudes, and costumes may be different but inside, people are basically the same. The world over, everybody

---

longs to be happy and fulfilled. They want to be loved. They all seek spiritual peace with God.

These radical young Muslim men were sincere. They prayed five times a day and fasted and prayed during Ramadan. They never ate pork, drank wine, used drugs, or smoked cigarettes. They were sincere Muslims who followed all the rules, yet they were sincerely wrong.

I didn't know they were in the crowd that night. If I had known, I might have run from them. Everyone thinks I'm so brave, but it's not that I am so brave, it's that I'm unaware. I had no idea what I was getting into. As I approached the microphone, Pastor Onyina, one of the local pastors, said, "Tommy, I need to tell you something."

"I can't talk now," I responded. "I'm getting ready to preach. I'm on next. I'm ready. I've got my game face on. I've got to go. Let me go!"

He said, "No! I've got to tell you something urgent."

So I reluctantly said, "Okay." We went over to a place in the back and he told me there was a Muslim gang present that night that wanted to kill me. Pastor Onyina exclaimed. "The last time someone preached here, they stoned him to death!"

I just smiled at him and said, "My dear friend, I love you like a brother. You're one of my oldest friends. I know you better than most of my own relatives. But the next time you have something to tell me before I preach, save it."

However, I took his warning to heart. One thing I did differently that night was I prayed with my eyes wide open. I was really *watching* and *praying*. I was ready. If someone threw a rock, I was going to dodge it.

I launched out and began preaching the Gospel. It was hard to preach. We were having equipment problems. Insects were flying up my nose and down my throat. As I was fighting with the sound system, I was losing my audience. Muslims in western Ghana have never been trained to sit still and listen to preaching. When their imams preach, they get up and talk, argue with each other, and walk around. It's chaotic!

I knew if they did not listen to the Gospel, they could not believe. And if they didn't believe, God would not confirm the message with miracles. Faith comes by hearing. The power of God is in the Gospel. I am not ashamed of the gospel of Christ, for it is the power of God unto salvation (Romans 1:16). I knew the people had to hear it in order to believe it, so I kept preaching the Gospel. I knew the Word of God spoken from my lips was like a sharp sword, piercing anything and penetrating into the deepest parts of the human heart.

By the end of the first service, my voice had diminished to a mere growl, yet it was time to pray. Oh, I prayed! I prayed for the multitude to receive the miracles of Jesus, even before I prayed for them to be saved, because I knew the crowd would need to see miracles before they would believe in Jesus. I gazed across the crowd and saw tens of thousands of people. The men were all dressed in Muslim robes and skullcaps. The women were all covered up in swaths of cloth. Interestingly, in Ghana, the Muslim women are not completely veiled. They have been trained *never* to look directly into a man's eyes because they have been taught that they are not worthy. Men don't consider them equal.

The first person to come up on the platform was a Muslim woman. She had been totally paralyzed; her legs were dead and useless. God had just given her a brand new pair of legs. I tried to look in her eyes and ask, "Are you happy?" but she wouldn't meet my gaze. She averted her eyes by bending low, so I went down too. She went down lower until we both went all the way down on the platform. Finally, we looked at each other, and a brilliant smile broke across her face and we stood up, looking into each other's eyes like equals.

It turned out that she was actually related to one of the radicals in the gang. He began weeping. The gang witnessed even more miracles. A girl who had been totally blind was healed. A blind woman who had come to the meeting, led by the hand by her brother, was healed. Oh how that brother and sister hugged each other, looking into each other's faces and weeping. Everyone who got healed was Muslim. Everyone who received Jesus said, "We are now no longer Muslims. Now we believe in Jesus."

It is impossible to even tell of even a fraction of the tremendous miracles God performed during that crusade. For ten days, we witnessed some of the most fantastic miracles we have ever seen. Each night, we prayed with thousands of sincere Ghanaians to receive Jesus Christ as their Lord and personal Savior. The intense hunger of the precious Ghanaian people and their boldness to turn from their strong cultural Muslim beliefs, witchcraft, and idol worship, was rewarded with joy and freedom.

After the first service, the gang came up to one of our team members and said, "We came here with the intention of killing that man. We were furious that he would come here and lie to our people. But now we have heard him speak and we have seen the miracles ourselves. Now we know that what he says is true and we are pleased." Of course, I was pleased that they were pleased. Needless to say, I was not stoned to death that night after all!

Chapter 10
Miracles Reveal

Miracles reveal the nature of God, which is love. God loves people. The number one reason God does miracles is because He doesn't want people to suffer. He created man and woman perfect and beautiful, pure and sinless, strong and healthy. That was His design.

God has been revealing Himself by supernatural wonders and fantastic manifestations of His power from the beginning, for the sole purpose of causing people to repent of their sin and follow Him again. He is a God of action and results. He is unchanging in His plan to win back the people He created. He has always been a God of miracles and He always will be. He is powerful, living, and full of compassion.

If Philip, Stephen, Peter, and the rest of the early church had the awesome power of God working through them so intensely, how much more should we, the modern body of Christ, have it working through us? Many eyes have grown dim. I pray fervently that our eyes will see with the eyes of Jesus: bright, keen, and clear.

As you read some more testimonies of God's miracle working power, rejoice with those who have been healed and brought into newness of life. Even if you never set foot in Africa, India, Asia or South America, you can still have a part in crusades like ours through your prayers and support. There is no victory without the sacrifice and hard work of many people behind the scenes.

A Typical, Miracle-Filled Crusade

On the first night of a crusade, I am often shocked to see the vast sea of people who have come to hear the Word of God and be healed. Huge soccer fields are packed with people shoulder-to-shoulder, standing together as far as the eye can see. You can feel the heat and see the dust, but most of all you can feel the desperation of the people. The bulk of the crowd is always made up of people lost without Christ, drawn in by the outlandish promises of healing.

Looking out on the crowd, you can always see those who are blind, who have been led by others to the crusade. The demon-possessed people are always there, most of them half-naked or dressed in rags, tormented, and crazed. Cripples hobble on crutches, dragging their useless and twisted limbs, or even scooting on their buttocks because they do not have the money for wheelchairs or medical treatment.

When I take the microphone, the fire of God burns hot within me to tell every person they can be free. I declare that every blind person can receive their sight, every person who is sick can become well in an instant, and every need can be met. I declare that everyone can live unafraid of the evil of demons and witchcraft. I preach the Good News of Jesus Christ usually a simple sermon about Jesus' life, death, and resurrection. Often I quote Hebrews 13:8 (NKJV), "Jesus Christ is the same yesterday, today, and forever."

Then after my sermon, I pray for everyone at once. I come against the evil spirits of infirmity and oppression. I rebuke the spirits of blindness, deafness, and insanity, and stand against every unclean spirit that brings people into bondage. I resist the spirits of paralysis and command them to loose the people in Jesus' name. At the end of the prayer, I simply thank God that He will stretch forth His Mighty hand once again, letting His power flow like fire, burning all traces of disease, curse, and weakness.

I declare, "Thank You for hearing me Lord!" Then I proclaim to the people that the power of God is healing them right now. I tell the cripples to rise up from the ground, hold up their crutches and walk. I tell the blind people to open up their eyes and see. I command the deaf to hear in Jesus' name. "Get up!" I say to the people. "Act on your faith! Your sickness is healed!"

There is a wave of excitement all through the crowd as many who are healed make their way to the platform, pushing with great effort through the press of the crowd. You can see ex-cripples holding their crutches and canes high in triumph as they walk, jump and praise God. Some of them are notable cripples, well known throughout the area. They bring their crutches and canes to the platform and throw them down joyfully.

When the healed people reach the platform, all heaven breaks loose! The people who used to be deaf can repeat every word I whisper in their ears. The people who used to be blind can point to whatever I tell them to look at. It is impossible to describe the joy of those who receive their healing. The great mass of people is overwhelmed by the miracles and heaven rejoices with all of us.

Dance Instructor Healed

At one crusade in Ghana, a former dance instructor received Christ, along with his healing. After he was healed, he could resume his livelihood. Ten years previously, Mr. A.K. Nyadzie had been a dance instructor. He loved his work and was very skillful at performing the local dances of Ghana. He was left crippled by a car accident and walked with great difficulty, leaning on a long staff while dragging his legs along.

Mr. Nyadzie saw some posters advertising our crusades and became very curious. He came to the crusade and listened to the message of Jesus. He was overwhelmed by God's great love and he believed in Jesus. When I led the people in the prayer of salvation, he received Jesus as his Savior. Then during the prayer for the sick, a sharp pain went through his legs. When the pain left, he felt strong and light. He threw away his staff and started dancing on the way to the platform. Once he reached the platform, he danced with me and all the pastors. Jesus' love had made him able to dance again with pure joy.

Juan in Tiquisate, Guatemala

Juan's leg was infected with gangrene and needed to be amputated. That was terrible enough, but to make things worse, he didn't have money for the operation. What could he do? He heard about our crusade so he came, truly in need of a real miracle from God. After I preached the Gospel and prayed, Juan received instant healing. He praised God as he gave his testimony.

This, however, was not the end of his story. After the healing miracle, he went back to his house and organized a huge party to celebrate his healing. He invited all his friends who were not believers, along with many others. About five hundred people came to his party. He gathered them all together and gave his testimony of how God healed him. They were amazed at this undeniable proof. Right then and there, many surrendered their lives to Jesus Christ and became brand-new believers. We saw Juan when we went to Tiquisate again. He was in perfect health. During that second crusade, we had him come up and give his dynamic testimony. God's miracles multiply!

Pioneers Blazing New Trails

Our ministry, Frontier Evangelism, is about being pioneers. We blaze new trails to the frontlines of Satan's turf. The word "pioneer" comes from the old French word *pionier* or *peonier*, which means foot soldier. A pioneer was someone who was sent by his commander into enemy territory, perilous and risky places, and often to the front lines of a battle. His job was to reach strategic targets, often behind enemy lines, to use his weapons to strike down the enemy and render his weapons useless.

That is exactly what we are in the spiritual realm, "Gospel pioneers." We go to the front lines, behind enemy territory and target the most heavily defended strongholds. When we arrive with the Gospel, the sword of the Spirit, and the inexorable force of the Holy Ghost, we leave the devil's kingdom in shambles.

New frontiers are all around us as we advance, holding campaign after campaign. The word *campaign* is defined as a series of organized military operations with a particular objective in a war. That is a good description of what we do in the spiritual war. Hallelujah! Jesus won the complete and utter victory over Satan and his demonic forces on the cross. The Bible says that "He too shared in their [our] humanity so that by his death he might break the power of him who holds the power of death—that is, the devil—and free those who all their lives were held in slavery by their fear of death" (Hebrews 2:14– 15, NIV; brackets mine).

We demonstrate Satan's defeat by the word of our testimony and by the blood of the Lamb, setting the captives free. We bring emancipation to tens of thousands, who all their lives have been vulnerable to the slavery of satanic influence. We organize strategic, aggressive operations in this battle for souls, blazing trails to remote cities, jungles, and the urban jungles of teeming cities. You, too, can be a pioneer for Christ, wherever He has placed you. Together, we all have the same objective: Bringing the Kingdom of God to rule over the human wildernesses of the earth—making people beautiful for Jesus!

Epilogue

The Road Less Traveled

Tue statement: Tommy O'Dell has seen more miracles in one day than most people will witness in a lifetime. The miracles started with my first prayer of surrender to Jesus and they have never stopped since. In the past ten years of our ministry, we have conducted more than seventy crusades in twenty-five nations. Our diverse audiences have ranged from the Hindus of India to the Juju practitioners of Africa. The Gospel message has been heard and believed by Muslims in Africa, Hindus in India, animists in primitive cultures, atheists in Europe, Roman Catholics in South America, and Protestants in Northern Ireland.

In each of our overseas meetings, crowds ranging from 30,000 to 150,000 gather around the platform to hear the Gospel's positive words of hope and healing. Then, before astonished eyes, the crippled walk, the deaf hear, the blind see, and the diseased are instantly and miraculously healed.

This ministry takes me on a road less traveled, and all such roads are narrow and dangerous. The narrow paths that meander through the jungles of Africa, India, and South America often lead to unknown peril. Sometimes my family accompanies me, but other times, concerned for their safety, I reluctantly entrust my wife Elisabeth and our five children to America's safe borders, while I go out to face the unknown by myself, pulling together a support team as I go.

If I were to declare, "God is healing you now!" in an American evangelistic meeting and nothing happened, the result would be mere disappointment. But in the wilderness of the Third World, I know that boasting of such miracles means that I am taking my life into my hands. If nothing happens, I can be killed for it. But I am always confident—whether I go far away from home to preach or just stay at home to write a newsletter—that Jesus, my Lord and Savior, will keep me safe. His power is irresistible. His love is contagious. Have you experienced it?

Prayer

Heavenly Father, we thank You for Your miracle resurrection life. Thank You for sending Jesus to be the pioneer of our faith in You. Thank You for Your amazing love, for the way You come to us, care about us, and never reject us when we come to You in faith.

Oh Lord, we stand on Your promises of salvation, healing, and deliverance. Thank You for honoring Your Word by confirming it with miracles, healing our friends, and manifesting Your love. We know You have compassion for our friends right now and that You are working in them, doing wonderful miracles right now, in Jesus' Name, Amen.

Harvest

(poem by Tommy Ray)

Multitudes in darkness, the stormy waves of the sea,

The end of all things approaching, and then eternity.

To give, to surrender all, to pick up the cross,

Carry it into waves of the forgotten, ravaged, and lost.

I see a harvest blowing and a fierce wind whirling.

I hear a shout of truth proclaimed against the storm's black hurling.

In Jesus' name the sea will calm, precious light pierce through,

To reach with healing beam of love, revealed to make all new.

Devils and curses and unholy beasts tremble when we stand

To share the Gospel secrets, and to break the chains and bands.

They flee in fright. The slaves are free, and sunrise shines with might.

Those who dwelt in death's shadow are translated into light.

We Need a Healing

by Tommy Ray O'Dell

We need a healing

Touched by Jesus' love

We need illumination

Redemption from above

Everything broken and fallen

Sinful and diseased

Needs freedom resurrection

Satisfaction guaranteed

We need a healing

We need a healing

Whole world knows what I'm feeling

Lord, Lord, Lord, Lord… We need a healing!

We need refreshing, Father, comfort

Rock my soul

We need rejuvenation

Nail torn hands can make me whole

Putting it all together

Rescued from the jaws of night

We need a healing, a healing, Passion's promise of delight

We need a healing

We need a healing

Whole world knows what I'm feeling

Lord, Lord, Lord, Lord… We need a healing!

Love Don't Strut

by Tommy Ray O'Dell

If I speak with human eloquence and angelic ecstasy, without love,

*I'm nothing...**but a noise maker.***

Or if I speak prophecies with power, revealing all mysteries, without love,

*I'm nothing...**but a word shaker.***

And if I have faith to say to a mountain, 'Jump! And he say how high?'
without love,

*I'm nothing... **but a soul faker.***

If I give everything I own to the poor, and my body to be burned at the
stake, without love,

*I ain't nothing... **but a praise taker.***

Love doesn't covet

Love never gives up

Love cares more about others

LOVE DON'T STRUT

Doesn't have a fat head

Ain't pushy or corrupt

Love ain't freakin' or buckin'

LOVE DON'T STRUT

Ain't obsessed with itself
Never locked in a rut
Doesn't get high on other people's blues
LOVE DON'T STRUT

Love is never plastic
Ain't lookin' for its cut
Ain't religious or judgmental
LOVE DON'T STRUT

Love takes pleasure in truth
Its door is never shut
Hopes, trusts and believes all things
LOVE DON'T STRUT

Champion
by Tommy Ray O'Dell

For many years I have been the knight of enchanted colors,
coloring things that, to me, needed some heightened allure.
I championed a cause,
I suppose that the poets had for long suffered, asking for philosopher's aide?
We were far too demure.
I use the royal, "we."
Romantic knight, jousting excessively at enemies of reason, logic and history
Romantic knight, defending the indefensible until I ended up flat on my
philosophy.
Some might cite poets as the delusion fiends that had enthralled me early;
but most of them through the ages have been far from unfair,
expressing the dark side of the scene.
The true fiends are the crazies who dabble at all arts and are masters of
none.
The true fiends are the lazies who, like middle age alchemists, yearn for gold.
The true fiends are the hazies who murk and muddle the waters of love.
Romantic knight, jousting excessively at enemies of reason, logic and history
Romantic knight, defending the indefensible until I ended up flat on my
philosophy
For many years: to be precise, a decade for every Christ year,
I wore my superstition like a robe.
Until the dark-age boy within declared, the emperor is naked and I awoke.

126

Zimbabwe: Cripple walks again to the glory of God. After Tommy Ray O'Dell preaches the Good News message to a crowd of tens of thousands, this man too, believes and begins to walk in Jesus' name!

Tommy Ray O'Dell, 18 years old in Lisburn, Northern Ireland. Right after receiving deliverance and salvation young Tommy Ray set out to tell people what Jesus has done for him.

In Hohoe, Ghana, West-Africa, a deaf & dumb school was brought to the miracle crusade by one of the teachers. The Lord touched them and healed them ALL. The next day Tommy Ray O'Dell walked to the school and checked each of the children's ears to make sure they have all received their hearing. Now the teachers have to teach them how to talk! Praise God!

Tommy Ray & Elisabeth O'Dell held their first healing campaigns in Central America. Tommy Ray O'Dell (19), here in Honduras, preaches the Gospel with faith and power. The Lord healed many including a woman with a paralyzed hand.

Tommy Ray O'Dell and interpreter Carmen, assist a boy in testifying how the Lord has healed his crippled leg.

Below left: in Ghana, this man listens to the Gospel Message in one of the Frontier Evangelism miracle campaigns. Tommy Ray O'Dell prays for the sick to be healed and God heals the man's legs. He can walk again!

Below right: Maxwell Mandela from Zimbabwe was in a devastating car accident years ago. He broke his back and the doctors told him he would spend the rest of his life in his wheelchair. But…because he has come to the great miracle crusade, he hears the message of the Cross, believes and is healed in the mighty name of Jesus Christ.

Miracle Working Faith

In the many Zimbabwe crusades held, many blind eyes received their sight including this dear man and precious woman!

On Borneo, one of the 1,500 islands of Indonesia, this precious Dayak lady received her hearing. She is so thankful Tommy Ray O'Dell traveled all the way to the other end of the world to bring her the Gospel Message. Below: sharing the Love of Jesus with two sweet ladies.

Blind, deaf and crippled Catherineis healed in Jesus' Name!

(Zimbabwe) Catherine Mahoa was blind, deaf and crippled! She was literally paralyzed in a dark prison where silence ruled. Try to imag¬ine the overwhelming joy and thankfulness she experiences right now! Jesus has come to her with

his precious love and mighty power, shining His glorious light into her dark¬ness. She is a walking, seeing and hearing miracle!

Frontier Evangelism Mass Miracle Festivals held around the world in
Zimbabwe, Ghana and India.

Top left: While walking one morning Tommy Ray O'Dell passed a village prayer meeting in a crude, mud-bricked home. He entered and spoke to the believers. Ariette was folded in half, paralyzed, unable to stand straight or walk. Tommy Ray laid hands on her, prayed in Jesus' name and left. Now she has come walking all the way from her village to testify that God has healed her! Top right: Moslem man, totally blind for many years is now praising and thanking God, "I can see! I can see!"

Mid right: 7 year old Ajala, was a deaf mute. Now she hears for the first time in her young life. Bottom right: Deaf mute from birth copies Tommy Ray O'Dell when he hears him clap. He is totally awestruck.

Above: Dear lady in Borneo has received her sight. She is overwhelmed by God's love and power.

Below: Guatemalan man receives sight for his right eye.

Maria Perez, the witch from Argentina stands here,

Tommy Ray O'Dell, a professional recording artist plays with the indigenous people of Ecuador in one of the Mass Miracle Festivals.

Shy Indian lady is filled with joy and thankfulness now that Jesus has opened her ears at the Mass Miracle Festival.

In the Netherlands this man followed Tommy Ray O'Dell to several locations, determined to get healed! Here he raises his cane triumphantly since Jesus has healed his legs, completely!

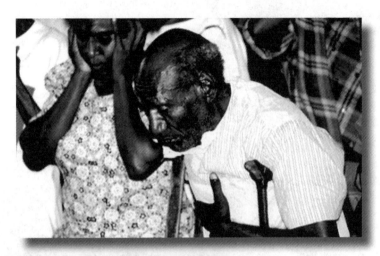

Papua New Guinea: While Tommy Ray O'Dell was praying for the crowd, this dear crippled man prays with all his heart. The next photos are of him completely healed. Jesus is a Miracle Worker!

Top: Boy's eye sees again! Below: Abuba Kari, a devout Moslem Hadji, has been blind for 30 years. "Tonight I believe that Jesus is the Son of God, risen from the dead. He is my Lord. I must believe because he has given me my sight."

Besides conducting Mass Miracle Festivals, Frontier Evangelism also holds Pastors and Leaders Seminars where thousands attend daily. Tommy Ray & Elisabeth O'Dell have made it their passion to reach people and change their lives for the better on every level: spirit, soul and body. They have given away countless tons of   food and necessities to prisons, refugee camps, cities and orphanages, worldwide.

"The Spirit of the Lord is on me, because he has anointed me to preach good news to the poor.He has sent me to proclaim freedom for the prisoners and recovery of sight for the blind, to release the oppressed,to proclaim the year of the Lord's favor." Luke 4:18 & 19

Left to right: Jesse & Deedee, Tommy Ray & Elisabeth, Donovan, Jerry, Madalena, Andresa & Tommy Lee.

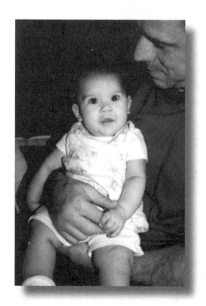

Grandfather Tommy Ray O'Dell, and first grandchild Genesis Anabella.

Frontier Evangelism Mass Miracle Festivals held around the world in Zimbabwe and Togo.

"Tommy Ray O'Dell lives with a deep compassion for the lonely, lost, hurting, sick, neglected peoples of the world. He is a powerful man who loves Jesus, and his world ministry makes him a distinguished evangelist. He and his wonderful wife, Elisabeth, and their precious family have really paid a great price to give the Gospel to the unreached."

–Dr. T.L Osborn

To contact the author:

Frontier Evangelism
8177 S Harvard Ave
Tulsa, OK 74137
www.tommyrayodell.org

PRAYER OF SALVATION

God loves you—no matter who you are, no matter what your past. God loves you so much that He gave His one and only begotten Son for you. The Bible tells us that "...whoever believes in Him shall not perish but have eternal life" (John 3:16 NIV). Jesus laid down His life and rose again so that we could spend eternity with Him in heaven and experience His absolute best on earth. If you would like to receive Jesus into your life, say the following prayer out loud and mean it from your heart.

Heavenly Father, I come to You admitting that I am a sinner. Right now, I choose to turn away from sin, and I ask You to cleanse me of all unrighteousness. I believe that Your Son, Jesus, died on the cross to take away my sins. I also believe that He rose again from the dead so that I might be forgiven of my sins and made righteous through faith in Him. I call upon the name of Jesus Christ to be the Savior and Lord of my life. Jesus, I choose to follow You and ask that You fill me with the power of the Holy Spirit. I declare that right now I am a child of God. I am free from sin and full of the right-eousness of God. I am saved in Jesus' name. Amen.

If you prayed this prayer to receive Jesus Christ as your Savior for the first time, please contact us on the Web at **www.harrisonhouse.com** to receive a free book.

Or you may write to us at
Harrison House • P.O. Box 35035 • Tulsa, Oklahoma 74153

The Harrison House Vision

Proclaiming the truth and the power

Of the Gospel of Jesus Christ

With excellence;

Challenging Christians to

Live victoriously,

Grow spiritually,

Know God intimately.